Allyn and Bacon
Special Education On the Net

Allyn and Bacon

Special Education
On the Net

2001 Edition

Judith Osgood Smith

Purdue University–Calumet

Doug Gotthoffer

California State University–Northridge

Allyn and Bacon

Boston • London • Toronto • Sydney • Tokyo • Singapore

Series Editor: Virginia Lanigan
Multimedia Editor: Nina Tisch
Cover Creative Director: Kate Conway
Cover Designer: Amy Braddock
Editorial Production Service: Omegatype Typography, Inc.

NOTICE: Between the time Web site information is gathered and then published, it is not unusual for some sites to have ceased operating. Also, the transcription of URLs can result in unintended typographical errors. The Publisher would appreciate notification where these occcur so that they may be corrected in subsequent editions. Thank you.

In its effort to provide a diverse list of Web sites, the Publisher has included links that do not necessarily represent the views of Allyn and Bacon. Faculty, students, and researchers are strongly advised to use their analytical skills to determine the truth, accuracy, and value of the content in individual Web sites.

TRADEMARK CREDITS: Where information was available, trademarks and registered trademarks are indicated below. When detailed information was not available, the publisher has indicated trademark status with an initial capital where those names appear in the text.

Macintosh is a registered trademark of Apple Computer, Inc.

Microsoft is a registered trademark of Microsoft Corporation. Windows, Windows95, Windows98, and Microsoft Internet Explorer are trademarks of Microsoft Corporation.

Netscape and the Netscape Communicator logo are registered trademarks of Netscape Communications Corporation.

ISBN 0-205-33153-X

Printed in the United States of America

10 9 8 7 6 5 4 3 2 1   03 02 01 00

Contents

Allyn and Bacon
Special Education On the Net

Introduction to the Internet

You're about to embark on an exciting experience as you become one of the millions of citizens of the Internet. Once you've accustomed yourself to this wonderful new world, you'll be amazed by how much you can discover, learn, and accomplish as you explore the Internet's dynamic resources.

Why Use the Internet?

In *Understanding Media,* Marshall McLuhan foresaw the existence of the Internet when he described electronic media as an extension of our central nervous system. On the other hand, today's students introduced to the Internet for the first time describe it as "cool."

No matter which description you favor, you are immersed in a period that is transforming the way we live by transforming the nature of the information we live by. As recently as 1980, intelligence was marked by "knowing things." If you were born in that year, by the time you were old enough to cross the street by yourself, that definition had changed radically. Today, in a revolution that makes McLuhan's vision tangible, events, facts, rumors, and gossip are distributed instantly to all parts of the global body. The effects are equivalent to a shot of electronic adrenaline. No longer the domain of the privileged few, information is shared by all the inhabitants of McLuhan's global village. Meanwhile, the concept of information as intelligence feels as archaic as a television remote control with a wire on it (ask your parents about that).

With hardly more effort than it takes to rub your eyes open in the morning, you can connect with the latest news, gossip about your favorite music group or TV star, learn the best places to eat on spring break, find out the weather back home, or follow the trials and tribulations of that soap opera character whose life conflicts with your history class. You can carry on a real-time conversation with your best friend at a college half a continent away, or play interactive games with a dozen or more world-wide challengers. And that's just for fun. When it comes to your education, newspaper and magazine archives are now almost instantly available, as are the contents of many reference books. Distant and seemingly unapproachable experts are found answering questions in discussion groups or electronic newsletters.

The Internet also addresses the major problem facing us in our split-second, efficiency-rated culture: Where do we find the time? The Internet allows professors and students to keep in touch, collaborate, and learn without placing unreasonable demands on individual schedules. Professors are posting everything from course syllabi to homework solutions and are increasingly answering questions online, all in an effort to ease the pressure for face-to-face meetings by supplementing them with cyberspace offices. The Internet enables students and professors to expand office hours into a twenty-four-hours-a-day, seven-days-a-week operation. Many classes have individual sites at which enrolled students can gather electronically to swap theories, ideas, resources, gripes, and triumphs.

By freeing us from the more mundane operations of information gathering, and by providing numerous diverse sources of information, the Internet encourages us to be more creative and imaginative. Instead of devoting most of our time to gathering information and precious little to analyzing and synthesizing it, the Internet tips the balance in favor of the skills that separate us from silicon chips. As much as the Internet ties us together, it simultaneously emphasizes our individual skills—our ability to connect information in new, meaningful, and exciting ways. Rarely have we had the opportunity to make connections and observations on such a wide range of topics, to create more individual belief systems, and to chart a path through learning that makes information personally useful and meaningful.

A Brief History of the Internet

The Internet began as a tool for national defense. In the mid-1960s, the U.S. Department of Defense was searching for an information analogy to

part

1

the new Interstate Highway System, a way to move computing resources around the country in the event the Cold War caught fire. The immediate predicament, however, had to do with the Defense Department's budget, and the millions of dollars spent on computer research at universities and think tanks. Much of these millions was spent on acquiring, building, or modifying large computer systems to meet the demands of the emerging fields of computer graphics, artificial intelligence, and multiprocessing (where one computer was shared among dozens of different tasks).

While the research was distributed across the country, the unwieldy, often temperamental, computers were not. This made it difficult for computer scientists at various institutions to share their work without duplicating each other's hardware. Wary of being accused of re-inventing the wheel, the Advanced Research Projects Agency (ARPA), the funding arm of the Defense Department, invested in the ARPANET, a private network that would allow disparate computer systems to communicate with each other. Researchers could remain among their colleagues at their home campuses while using computing resources at government research sites thousands of miles away.

A small group of ARPANET citizens soon began writing computer programs to perform little tasks across the Internet. Most of these programs, while ostensibly meeting immediate research needs, were written for the challenge of writing them. These programmers, for example, created the first email systems. They also created games such as "Space Wars" and "Adventure." Driven in large part by the novelty and practicality of email, businesses and institutions accepting government research funds begged and borrowed their way onto the ARPANET, and the number of connections swelled.

As the innocence of the 1960s gave way to the business sense of the 1980s, the government eased out of the networking business, turning the ARPANET (now Internet) over to its users. While we capitalize the word "Internet," it may surprise you to learn there is no "Internet, Inc." in charge of this uniquely postmodern creation. Administration of this world-wide communication complex is still handled by the cooperating institutions and regional networks that comprise the Internet. The word "Internet" denotes a specific interconnected network of networks, not a corporate entity.

The emergence of the World Wide Web, developed by the European Laboratory for Particle Physics in the early 1990s, transformed the Internet. For the first time, images as well as text could be viewed through the aid of graphical Web browsers (software for navigating the Web).

part

1

Today, sophisticated browsers such as Netscape Navigator and Microsoft Internet Explorer have led to the Web's vast popularity.

Some Things You Ought to Know

In order to access the Internet, you must first have an Internet Service Provider (ISP). That's the organization providing you with your Internet account. Most of the time your ISP will be your school; but you may contract with one of the commercial providers such as America Online, Mindspring, the Microsoft Network, Earthlink, or AT&T.

Much of the confusion over the Internet comes from two sources. One is terminology. Just as the career you're preparing for has its own special vocabulary, so does the Internet. You'd be hard pressed to join in the shoptalk of archeologists, librarians, or carpenters if you didn't speak their language. Don't expect to plop yourself down in the middle of the Internet without some buzzwords under your belt, either. This chapter will explain the most common terms, but keep in mind that new Internet technologies are developing all the time.

The second source of confusion is that there are often many ways to accomplish the same ends on the Internet. This is a direct by-product of the freedom so highly cherished by Net citizens. When someone has an idea for doing something, he or she puts it out there and lets the Internet community decide its merits. As a result, it's difficult to put down in writing the *one exact* way to send email, search for information, or whatever.

There are also differences in the workings of a PC or Mac and the various versions of the two major Web browsers, Netscape Communicator (which contains Netscape Navigator as well as other software) and Microsoft Internet Explorer. If you can't find a particular command or function mentioned in the book, chances are it's there, but in a different place or with a slightly different name. Check the manual or online help that came with your computer, or ask a more computer-savvy friend or professor.

For example, this book covers Netscape 4.73. However, Netscape 6 is currently in preparation. It is said to be so different that version 5 has been skipped altogether! Netscape 6 will be easier to install and customize, with much smaller file sizes. Advanced search technology will make searches more accurate. New privacy options will be available for enhanced security. It will be possible to translate Web pages into another language almost instantly. Netscape 6 will allow multiple email accounts, including America Online email, and will automatically store contact information in an address book.

If learning about the Internet is making you a little nervous, relax! Getting up to speed takes a little time, but the effort will be well rewarded. Approach learning your way around the Internet with the same enthusiasm and curiosity you approach learning your way around a new college campus. This isn't a competition. Nobody's keeping score. And the only winner will be you.

Introducing the World Wide Web

If you've never seriously used the Web, you are about to take your first steps on what can only be described as an incredible journey. Just as no one owns the Internet, there is no formal organization among the collection of hundreds of thousands of computers that make up the part of the Net called the World Wide Web.

Initially, you might find it convenient to think of the Web as cable television with millions of channels. It's safe to say that, among all these channels, there's something for you to watch. Only, how do you find it? You could click through the channels one by one, of course, but by the time you found something of interest it would either (1) be over or (2) leave you wondering if there wasn't something better on that you're missing.

A more efficient way to search for what you want would be to consult some sort of TV listing. While you could skim through pages more rapidly than channels, the task would still be daunting. A more creative approach would allow you to press a button on your remote control that would connect you to a channel of interest; what's more, that channel would contain the names (or numbers) of other channels with similar programs. Those channels in turn would contain information about other channels. Now you could zip through this million-channel universe, touching down only at programs of potential interest.

If you have a feel for how this might work for television, you have a feel for what it's like to journey around (or "surf") the Web. Instead of channels, we have *Web sites*. Each site contains one or more *pages*. Each page may contain links to other pages, either in the same site or in other sites, anywhere in the world. These other pages may elaborate on the information you're looking at, direct you to related but not identical information, or even provide contrasting or contradictory points of view. And, of course, these pages could have links of their own.

Today, Web sites are maintained by businesses, institutions, affinity groups, professional organizations, government departments, and ordinary people anxious to express opinions, share information, sell products, or provide services. Because these sites are stored electronically, updating them is more convenient and practical than updating printed media. That makes Web sites far more dynamic than other types of research material you may be used to, and it means a visit to a Web site can open up new opportunities that weren't available as recently as a few hours ago.

Hypertext and Links

The invention that unveils these revolutionary possibilities is called *hypertext*. Hypertext is a technology for combining text, graphics, sounds, video, and links on a single World Wide Web page. Unlike traditional linear documents such as books, hypertext allows navigation through pages in any order that you like. Click on a link and you're transported, like Alice falling down the rabbit hole, to a new page, a new address, a new environment for research and communication.

Links come in three flavors: text, picture, and hot spot. A text link may be a letter, a word, a phrase, a sentence, or any contiguous combination of text characters. You can identify text links at a glance because the characters are <u>underlined</u> and often displayed in a unique color, setting the link apart from the rest of the text on the page. Picture links may be drawings, photos, or other graphic elements. On the Web, a picture may not only be worth a thousand words, but also the start of a journey into a whole new corner of cyberspace.

The hot spot is neither underlined nor bordered. It would be impossible to see were it not for a Web convention that offers you (literally) a helping hand for finding all types of links. Whenever the mouse cursor passes over a link, the cursor changes from an arrow to a hand. Wherever you see the hand icon, you can click and retrieve another Web page. Sweep the cursor over an area of interest, see the hand, follow the link, and you're surfing the Web. Hot spots are sometimes located on areas of a large picture called an "image map." Clicking on different areas of the image map will lead you to different Web pages.

In the Name of the Page

Zipping around the Web in this way may seem exciting, even serendipitous, but it's also fraught with peril. How, for instance, do you revisit a page of particular interest? Or share a page with a classmate? Or cite a

part

1

Text
Link

Picture
Link

Text links are underlined and set off in color. Picture links are set off by a colored border. Hot spots carry no visual identification.

page as a reference for a professor? Web page designers assign titles to their pages; unfortunately, there's nothing to prevent two designers from assigning the same title to different pages.

An instrument that uniquely identifies Web pages does exist. It's called a *Universal Resource Locator (URL)*. A URL contains all the information necessary to locate the:

- Web page containing the information you're looking for;
- computer that hosts (stores) that page of information;
- form in which the information is stored.

A typical URL looks like this:

```
http://www.abacon.com/index.html
```

You enter it into the **Location** or **Address** field at the top of your browser window. Hit the **Return** (or **Enter**) key, and your browser will deliver to your screen the exact page specified. When you click on a link, you're actually using a shorthand alternative to typing the URL yourself because the browser does it for you. In fact, if you watch the "Location" or "Address" field when you click on a link, you'll see its contents change to the URL to which you're traveling.

The URL Exposed

How does your browser know where you're going? As arcane as the URL appears, there is a logical explanation to its apparent madness. This is true not only of URLs, but also of computers in general. Because a computer's "intelligence" only extends to following simple instructions exactly, most of the commands, instructions, and procedures you'll encounter have simple underlying patterns. Once you familiarize yourself with these patterns, you'll find you're able to make major leaps in your understanding of new Internet features.

To unscramble the mysteries of Web addresses, we'll start at the end of the URL and work our way toward the front.

```
/index.html
```

This is the name of a single file or document. Eventually, the contents of this file/document will be transferred over the Internet to your computer. However, because there are undoubtedly thousands of files on the Internet with this name, we need to clarify our intentions a bit more.

```
www.abacon.com
```

This is the name of a particular Internet *Web server,* a computer whose job it is to forward Web pages to you on request. By Internet convention, this name is unique. The combination of

```
www.abacon.com/index.html
```

identifies a unique file/document on a unique Web server on the World Wide Web. No other file has this combined address, so there's no question about which file/document to transfer to you.

The characters *http://* at the beginning of the URL identify the method by which the file/document will be transferred. The letters stand for HyperText Transfer Protocol.

You Can Go Home (and to Other Pages) Again

You know that a URL uniquely identifies a Web page and that links let you travel from page to page, but what if you end up at a dead end? Missing page messages take several forms, such as "URL 404," "Object not on this server," "Missing Object," or "Page Not Found," but they all tell you that the page specified by the link or URL no longer exists.

Quick Check

Don't Be Lost In (Hyper)Space

Let's pause for a quick check of your Web navigation skills. Look at the sample Web page below. How many links does it contain?
Did you find four? The four links include:

1. The word "links" in the second line below the seaside picture;

2. The sentence "What about me?";

3. The word "cyberspace" in the quick brown fox sentence;

4. The hot spot in the seaside picture. We know there's at least one link in the picture, because the cursor appears as a hand. (There may be more hot spots on the page, but we can't tell from this picture alone.)

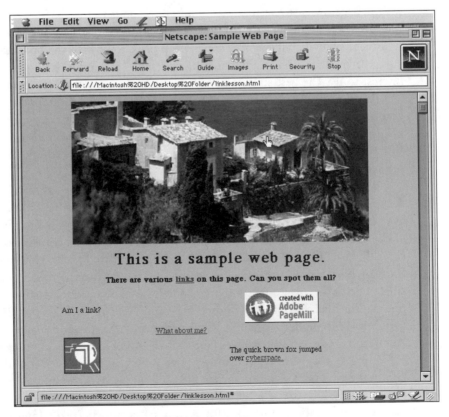

A sample web page to exercise your link identifying skills.

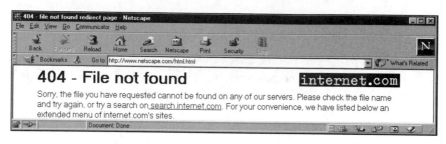

A missing page message, an all too common road hazard on the information superhighway.

There are many reasons for missing pages. You may have entered the URL incorrectly (every character must be precise and no spaces are allowed). More than likely, though, especially if you arrived here via a link, the page you're after has been moved or removed. Remember, anybody can create a link to any page. That's the good news. The bad news is that the owner of a page is under no obligation to inform the owners of links pointing to it that the page location has changed. In fact, there's no way for the page owner to even know about all the links to that page. Yes, the Internet's spirit of independence proves frustrating sometimes, but you'll find these small inconveniences are a cheap price to pay for the benefits you receive. Philosophy aside, though, we're still stuck on a page of no interest to us. The best strategy is to back up and try another approach.

Every time you click on the **Back** button at the top of the browser, you return to the previous page visited. That's because your browser keeps track of the pages you visit and the order in which you visit them. The **Back** button, and its counterpart, the **Forward** button, allow you to retrace the steps of your cyberpath.

What if you want to move two, three, or a dozen pages at once? Although you can click the **Back** or **Forward** buttons multiple times, Web browsers offer an easier navigation shortcut. If you use Netscape, clicking on the **Go** menu in the menu bar displays a list of your most recently visited pages, in the order in which you visited them. Unlike the **Back** or **Forward** buttons, you can select any page from the menu, and a single click takes you directly there. There's no need to laboriously move one page a time. If you use Internet Explorer, you can click on the **History** button in the Explorer bar or press the arrow at the end of the Address bar to see a list of links you visited in previous days and weeks.

Suppose you want to return to a page hours, days, or even months later. One way is to write down the URL of every page you may want to revisit. There's got to be a better way, and there is: We call them *bookmarks* (in Netscape Communicator) or *favorites* (in Microsoft Internet Explorer).

Like their print book namesakes, bookmarks (and favorites) flag specific Web pages. Selecting an item from the **Bookmark/Favorites** menu, like selecting an item from the **Go** menu, is the equivalent of entering a URL into the **Location** field of your browser, except that items in the **Bookmark/Favorites** menu are ones you've added yourself and represent pages visited over many surfing experiences, not just the most recent one.

To select a page from your bookmark list, pull down the **Bookmark/Favorites** menu and click on the desired entry. To save a favorite page location, use the Add feature available in both browsers. In Netscape Communicator, clicking on the **Add Bookmark** command makes a bookmark entry for the current page. **Add to Favorites** performs the same function in Internet Explorer. Clicking this feature adds the location of the current page to your **Bookmark/Favorites** menu.

A cautionary note is in order here. Your bookmark or favorites list physically exists only on your personal computer, which means that if you connect to the Internet on a different computer, your list won't be available. If you routinely connect to the Internet from a computer lab, there is a way to avoid the work of retyping your URLs each time you use a different computer. Both Internet Explorer and Netscape Navigator provide procedures to save favorites in a computer file that you can move from one computer to another.

In Internet Explorer, choose File Import and Export. Follow the on-screen instructions to Export Favorites. Insert a blank diskette into the diskette drive and choose the diskette drive when asked where you want the favorites exported. When you begin working on a different computer, insert your diskette with the file of favorites into the diskette drive. Again choose File, Open, and Browse. Locate the filename of your favorites in the browser window and open it. Your favorites will appear on screen as a list of links.

In Netscape, click on Bookmarks, and then Edit Bookmarks. (On the Mac, open the Communicator menu and choose Bookmarks). Open the File menu and choose Save As. Insert a blank diskette into the diskette drive and choose the diskette drive when asked where you want the bookmark file saved. When you begin working on a different computer, insert your diskette with the file of favorites into the diskette drive. Click on Bookmarks, and then Edit Bookmarks. (On the Mac, open the Communicator menu and choose Bookmarks). Click on File, Open Bookmarks File. Locate the filename of your bookmarks in the browser window and open it. Your bookmark file will now open when you choose Bookmarks.

Quick Check

As a quick review, here's what we know about navigating the Web so far:

- Enter a URL directly into the Location field;
- Click on a link;
- Use the **Back** or **Forward** icons;
- Select a page from the **Go** menu.
- Add bookmarks or favorite URLs.

Searching and Search Engines

Returning to our cable television analogy, you may recall that we glossed over the question of how we selected a starting channel in the first place. With a million TV channels, or several million Web pages, we can't depend solely on luck guiding us to something interesting.

On the Web, we solve the problem with specialized computer programs called *search engines* that crawl through the Web, page by page, cataloging its contents. As different software designers developed search strategies, entrepreneurs established Web sites where any user could find pages containing particular words and phrases. Today, Web sites such as Yahoo! offer you a "front door" to the Internet that begins with a search for content of interest.

The URLs for some popular search sites are:

AltaVista	www.altavista.com
Excite	www.excite.com
Google	www.google.com
HotBot	www.hotbot.com
Infoseek	www.infoseek.com
MetaCrawler	www.metacrawler.com
WebCrawler	www.webcrawler.com
Yahoo!	www.yahoo.com

Internet Gold Is Where You Find It

Let's perform a simple search using HotBot to find information about the history of the Internet. See the results in the screens shown below and on pages 14–16.

Out of curiosity, let's try our history of the Internet search using a different search engine. When we search for the phrase "history of the internet" using WebCrawler, the quotation marks serve the same purpose as selecting "the exact phrase" option in HotBot. But the Web-Crawler search only finds approximately 900 hits. Some are the same as those found using HotBot, some are different. Different searching strategies and software algorithms make using more than one search engine a must for serious researchers.

The major search engines conveniently provide you with tips to help you get the most out of their searches. These include ways to use AND and OR to narrow down searches, and ways to use NOT to eliminate unwanted hits.

part

1

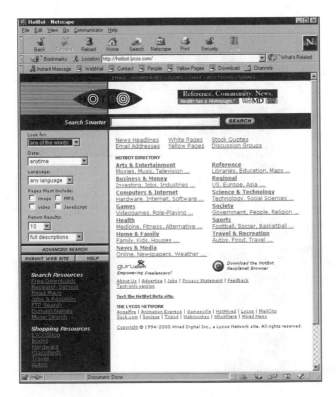

We'll start by searching for the words "internet" or "history." By looking for "any of the words," the search will return pages on which either "internet" or "history" or both appear.

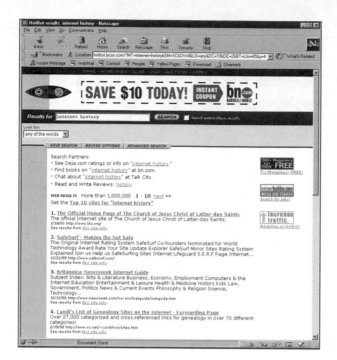

Our search returned more than 1,000,000 matches or *hits*. Pages are ranked according to the following factors: words in the title, keyword meta tags, word frequency in the document, and document length.

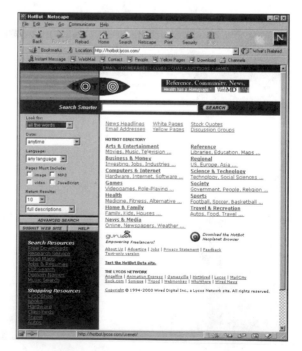

We can conduct the same search, but this time look for "all the words." The search will return hits when both "internet" and "history" appear on the same page, in any order, and not necessarily next to each other.

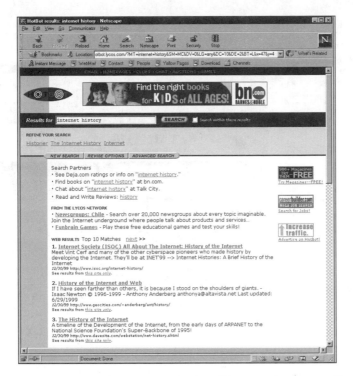

The search is narrowed down somewhat, but still has more than 1,000,000 hits.

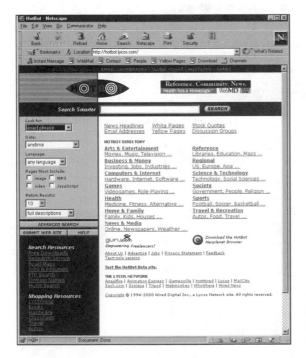

When we search for the exact phrase "internet history," which means those two words in exactly that order, with no intervening words, we're down to several thousand hits (still a substantial number).

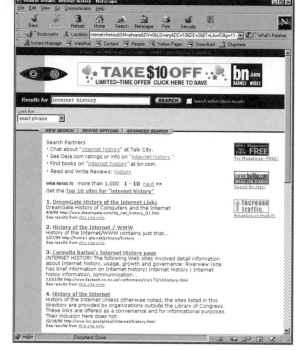

Now the first hits may be more specific. However, other hits in the list may have nothing to do with the history of the Internet. Hits happen. No search engine is 100 percent accurate 100 percent of the time. Spurious search results are the serendipity of the Internet. Look at them as an opportunity to explore something new.

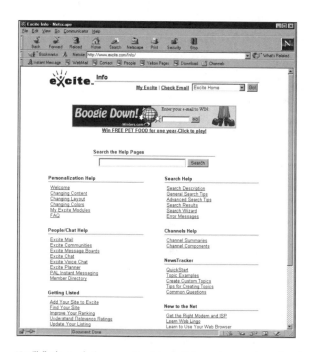

You'll find search tip pages like this at all the major search engine sites.

Each search engine also uses a slightly different approach to cataloging the Web, so your results may vary. Often, one search engine provides better results (more relevant hits) in your areas of interest; sometimes the wise strategy is to provide the same input to several different engines. No one search engine does a perfect job all the time, so experience will dictate the one that's most valuable to you.

http://www.excite.com/info

Quick Check

Let's review our searching strategies:

- ■ Visit one of the search engine sites;
- ■ Enter key words or phrases that best describe the search criteria;
- ■ Narrow the search if necessary by using options such as "all the words" or "the exact phrase." On some search engines, you may use the word "and" or the symbol "|" to indicate words that all must appear on a page;
- ■ Try using the same criteria with different search engines.

Additional Internet Resources

Developed by the University of Minnesota, **Gopher** was an early method for navigating the Internet. Where did it get its name? Some say a gopher was the university's mascot, but the name also sounds like "go for." And what you go for are files at a Gopher site. The contents are listed in a hierarchical menu with folders containing files. Text files can be read in a window. Gopher sites are still run by some universities. You can use your Web browser to connect by typing gopher://*name of site* in the location box.

Telnet is a program used to access remote databases, library catalogs, and MUDs/MOOs (discussed later in this chapter). Telnet uses Unix commands and is not very user-friendly. Some universities have telnet sites that require you to have an account on their server. Other sites let you log in as a guest. You can access a telnet site with your Web browser by typing telnet://*address of site*. A menu of options will appear.

File Transfer Protocol (FTP) is a method for sending (*uploading*) and receiving (*downloading*) files over the Internet. These files may be free software, text, graphics, audio, or video. Anonymous FTP sites allow anyone to log in as "anonymous" and use an email address as a password. For a list of FTP sites and tutorials, see FTPplanet.com at www.ftpplanet.com.

To access an FTP site with your Web browser, just enter the address in the location box by typing ftp://*address of site*. Once you are connected, you will see a directory listing with folder icons and document files. Special FTP client programs make it easy to send and receive files, or to transfer more than one file at a time. They are often used for managing Web sites. An example is WS_FTP, which you can download at www.ipswitch.com/pd_wsftp.html.

Plug-Ins Bring the Web to Life

Plug-ins are free software that allow Web pages to include audio, video, or animation. Some plug-ins, such as RealPlayer (audio and video) and Netscape Radio (live radio), are now included with Netscape. Others must be downloaded and installed before they can be used. These files may be compressed and need a utility program such as WinZip for Windows (www.winzip.com) or Stuffit for the Mac (www.aladdinsys.com) to decompress them.

part

1

Here are five plug-ins and where to get more information:

- Macromedia ShockWave makes it possible to view complex anima-
  tions and engage in interactions with the software. See www.macro-
  media.com/shockwave.
- RealAudio compresses audio files and transmits them over the Internet. It uses a technique called "streaming audio" so that the sound
  will start to play while the file is still downloading. The RealAudio
  Player appears in a separate window on your monitor. See
  www.realaudio.com.
- QuickTime Video was developed by Apple Computer, Inc. The
  QuickTime Player lets you play video files. There are versions for
  both the PC and the Mac. See quicktime.apple.com.
- The Macromedia Flash Viewer enables you to view animated text or
  graphics. It is also used for animated slide shows, games, and educational interactions. See www.macromedia.com.
- The Adobe Acrobat Viewer lets you view and print files created in
  Adobe Portable Document Format, a way of storing pages with
  complex layout. See
  www.adobe.com/products/acrobat/readermain.html.

part

1

Give Your Web Browser Some Personality—Yours

Email and newsgroups let you communicate with others through the
Internet at your own pace and on your own time. Before you can access
these functions, however, you must set up or personalize your browser.
If you always work on the same computer, this is a one-time operation
that takes only a few minutes. In it, you tell your browser where to find
essential computer servers, along with personal information the Internet
needs to move messages for you.

Step 1: Open the **Preferences** menu in Netscape Communicator or
the **Internet Options** in Microsoft Internet Explorer. In Netscape
the Preferences menu is located under the **Edit** menu; in Internet
Explorer the Internet Options can be found under the **Tools** menu.

Step 2: In Netscape Communicator, click on Mail and Newsgroups.
Tell the browser who you are and where to find your mail servers.
Your Reply To address is typically the same as your email address,

though if you have an email alias you can use it here. Microsoft Internet Explorer has slots for your mail servers in the same window. Your ISP will provide the server names and addresses. Be sure to use your username (and not your alias) in the "Account Name" field. SMTP handles your outgoing messages, while the POP3 server routes incoming mail. Often, but not always, these server names are the same. Netscape Communicator has a separate window for server names.

Step 3: Tell the browser where to find your news server. Your ISP will furnish the name of the server. Note that in Internet Explorer, you specify a helper application to read the news. Now that most computers come with browsers already loaded onto the hard disk, you'll find that these helper applications are already set up for you.

Step 4: Indicate your desired home page. For convenience, you may want your browser to start by fetching your favorite search site or your school library's home page. Enter the URL for this starting page in the home page address field. Both Netscape and Internet Explorer offer the option of "no home page" when you start up. In that case, you will get a blank browser window.

part

1

The Preferences or Options menu also lets you set up Web preferences such as the color of links and visited links (the default is blue and purple), style and size of fonts, history (how long to keep a list of pages you've visited), and advanced options such as security issues.

Operating systems such as Mac OS 8 and Microsoft Windows 95 and 98 offer automated help in setting up your browsers for Web, mail, and newsgroup operation. You need to know the names of the servers mentioned above, along with your username and other details, such as the address of the domain name server (DNS) of your ISP. You should receive all this information when you open your Internet account. If not, ask for it.

The (E)mail Goes Through

Email was one of the first applications created for the Internet by its designers. Your electronic Internet mailbox is to email what a post office box is to "snail mail" (the name Net citizens apply to ordinary, hand-delivered mail). This mailbox resides on the computer of your ISP. The Internet doesn't deliver a message to your door but instead leaves it in a conveniently accessible place (your mailbox) in the post office (the computer of your ISP), until you retrieve the mail using your combination (password).

If you currently have access to the Internet, your school or ISP assigned you a *username* (also called a user id, account name, or account number). This username may be your first name, your first initial and the first few characters of your last name, or some strange combination of numbers and letters only a computer could love. An email address is a combination of your username and the unique address of the computer through which you access your email. For example:

```
username@computername.edu
```

The three letters after the dot, in this case "edu," identify the top level "domain." There are six common domain categories in use: edu (educational), com (commercial), org (organization), net (network), mil (military), and gov (government). The symbol "@"—called the "at" sign—serves two purposes: For computers, it provides a neat, clean separation between your username and the computer name; for people, it makes Internet addresses more pronounceable. Your address is read: username "at" computer name "dot" e-d-u. Suppose your Internet username is "a4736g" and your ISP is Allyn & Bacon, the publisher of this book. Your email address might look like

part
1

```
a4736g@abacon.com
```

and you would tell people your email address is "ay-four-seven-three-six-gee at ay bacon dot com."

We Don't Just Handle Your Email, We're Also a Client

You use email with the aid of special programs called *mail clients*. As with search engines, mail clients have the same set of core features, but your access to these features varies with the type of program. On both the PC and the Mac, Netscape Communicator and Microsoft Internet Explorer give you access to mail clients while you're plugged into the Web. That way you can pick up and send mail while you're surfing the Web. The basic email service functions are creating and sending mail, reading mail, replying to mail, and forwarding mail. First we'll examine the process of sending and reading mail, and then we'll discuss how to set up your programs so that your messages arrive safely.

Let's look at a typical mail client screen, in this case from Netscape Communicator. You reach this screen by choosing **Messenger** from the

New message form, with fields for
recipient's address and the subject, and
a window for the text of the message.

Communicator menu. To send a message, choose the **New Msg** button to create a blank message form, which has fields for the recipient's address, the subject, and a window for the text of the message.

Fill in the recipient's address in the "To" field, just above the arrow. Use your own address. We'll send email to ourselves and use the same message to practice sending email and reading it as well; then you'll know if your messages come out as expected. Click in the "Subject" field and enter a word or phrase that generally describes the topic of the message. Since we're doing this for the first time, let's type "Maiden Email Voyage." Click anywhere in the text window and enter your message: "Hi. Thanks for guiding me through sending my first email." You'll find that the mail client works here like a word processing program, which means you can insert and delete words and characters and highlight text.

Now click the **Send** button on the Navigation toolbar. You've just created and sent your first email message. In most systems, it takes from a few seconds to a few minutes for a message to yourself to reach your mailbox, so you might want to take a short break before continuing. When you're ready to proceed, close the **Composition** window and click the **Get Msg** button.

What Goes Around Comes Around

Now let's retrieve the message you just sent to yourself. When retrieving mail, most mail clients display a window showing the messages in your mailbox and telling you how many new messages have been added.

If you've never used your email before, chances are that your message window is empty, or contains only one or two messages (usually official messages from the ISP) besides the one you sent to yourself. The message to yourself should be accompanied by an indicator of some sort—a colored mark, the letter N—indicating it's a new message. You also get to see the date of the message, who sent it, and the information you entered in the subject line. The Subject field lets you scan your messages and determine which ones you want to look at first.

The summary of received messages tells you everything you need to know about a message except what's in it. Click anywhere on the line to see the contents in the message window. Click on the message from yourself and you'll see the contents of the message displayed in a window. The information at the top—To, From, Subject, and so forth—is called the *header*. Depending on your system, you may also see some cryptic lines with terms such as X-Mailer, received by, and id number. Most of the time, there's nothing of interest in this part of the header, so just skip over it for now.

part

1

Moving Forward

The contents, or text, of your message can be cut and pasted just like any other text document. If you and a classmate are working on a project together, your partner can write part of a paper and email it to you, and you can copy the text from your email message and paste it into your word processing program.

What if there are three partners in this project? One partner sends you a draft of the paper for you to review. You like it and want to send it on to your other partner. The **Forward** feature lets you send the message intact, so you don't have to cut and paste it into a new message window.

To forward a message, highlight it in the Inbox (top) and click the Forward icon. Enter the recipient's address in the "To" field of the message window. Note that the subject of the message is "Fwd:" followed by the subject of the original message. Use the text window to add your comments ahead of the original message.

A Chance to Reply

Email is not a one-way message system. Let's walk through a reply to a message from a correspondent named Elliot. Highlight the message in your **Inbox** again, and this time click on the **Reply** icon. Depending on which program you're using, you'll see that each line in the message is preceded by either a vertical bar or a right angle bracket (>).

Note that the "To" and "Subject" fields are filled in automatically with the address of the sender and the original subject preceded by "Re:". In Internet terminology, the message has been *quoted*. The vertical bar or > is used to indicate lines written by someone else (in this case, the message's original author). Why bother? Because this feature allows you to reply without retyping the parts of the message to which you're responding. Because your typing isn't quoted, your answers stand out from the original message. Netscape Communicator 4.7 adds some blank lines above and below your comments, a good practice for you if your mail client doesn't do this automatically.

part
1

A Discussion of Lists

There's no reason you can't use email to create a discussion group. You pose a question, for example, by sending an email message to everyone in the group. Somebody answers and sends the answer to everyone else on the list, and so on. At least that's the theory.

In practice, this is what often happens. As people join and leave the group, you and the rest of your group are consumed with updating your lists, adding new names and deleting old ones. As new people join, their addresses may not make it onto the lists of all the members of the group, so different participants get different messages. The work of administering the lists becomes worse than any value anyone can get out of the group, and so it quickly dissolves.

Generally, you're better off letting the computer handle discussion group administration. A *listserv* or *electronic mailing list* is a program for administering email to lists of subscribers. It automatically adds and deletes list members and handles the distribution of messages.

Thousands of mailing lists have already been formed by users with common interests. You may find mailing lists for celebrities, organizations, political interests, occupations, and hobbies. Your instructor may establish a mailing list for your course. For a list of searchable listservs,

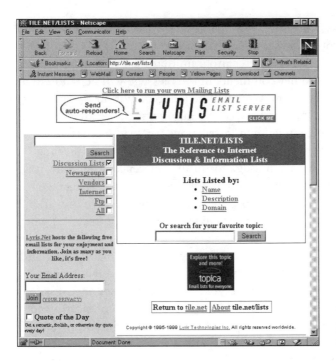

Tile.Net offfers shortcuts to working your way through the Internet's maze of discussion lists.

see www.liszt.com. Listservs come in several different flavors. Some are extremely active. You can receive as many as forty or more email messages a day. Other lists may send you a message a month. One-way lists, such as printed newsletters, do not distribute your reply to any other subscriber. Some lists distribute replies to everyone. These lists include mediated lists, in which an "editor" reviews each reply for suitability (relevance, tone, use of language) before distributing the message, and unmediated lists, in which each subscriber's response is automatically distributed to all the other subscribers with no restrictions except those dictated by decency and common sense, though these qualities may not always be obvious from reading the messages.

Get on a List Online

You join in the discussion by subscribing to a listserv, which is as straightforward as sending email. You need to know only two items: the name of the list and the address of the listserv program handling subscriptions.

To join a list, send a **Subscribe** message to the listserv administrative address (not necessarily the same as the listserv address, as the administrative address may serve a number of different lists). The message is usually as simple as "subscribe," the name of the list, and your name (your real name, not your username), all on one line. *And that's all.* This message will be read by a computer program that looks for these items only. At the very best, other comments in the message will be ignored; at the very worst, your entire message will be ignored. Within a few hours to a day after subscribing, the listserv will automatically send you a confirmation email message, including instructions for sending messages, finding out information about the list and its members, and canceling your subscription. Save this message for future reference. That way, if you do decide to leave the list, you won't have to circulate a message to the members asking how to unsubscribe, and you won't have to wade through fifty replies all relaying the same information you received when you joined.

Soon after your confirmation message appears in your mailbox, and depending on the activity level of the list, you'll begin receiving email messages. When you reply to a message, reply to the listserv address, not the address of the sender (unless you want your communication to remain private). The listserv program takes care of distributing your message listwide. Use the address in the "Reply To" field of the message. Most mail clients automatically use this address when you select the **Reply** command. Some may ask if you want to use the reply address (say yes). Some lists will send a copy of your reply to you so you know your message is online. Others don't send the author a copy, relying on your faith in the infallibility of computers.

You can cancel your subscription at any time. Simply send a message to the address you used to subscribe (which you'll find on that confirmation message you saved for reference), with "unsubscribe," followed on the same line by the name of the list. For example, to leave a list named "WRITER-L," you would send:

```
unsubscribe WRITER-L
```

Even if you receive messages for a short while afterwards, be patient—they will disappear.

Waste Not, Want Not

Listservs create an excellent forum for people with common interests to share their views; however, from the Internet standpoint, these lists are terribly wasteful. First of all, if there are a thousand subscribers to a list, every message must be copied a thousand times and distributed over the

part

1

Internet. If there are forty replies a day, this one list creates forty thousand email messages. Ten such lists mean almost a half million messages, most of which are identical, flying around the Net.

Another wasteful aspect of listservs is the way in which messages are answered. The messages in your mailbox on any given day represent a combination of new topics and responses to previous messages. But where are these previous messages? If you saved them, they're in your email mailbox taking up disk space. If you haven't saved them, you have nothing to which to compare the response. What if a particular message touches off a chain of responses, with subscribers referring not only to the source message but to responses as well? It sounds like the only safe strategy is to save every message from the list, a suggestion as absurd as it is impractical.

What we really need is something closer to a bulletin board than a mailing list. On a bulletin board, messages are posted once. Similar notices wind up clustered together. Everyone comes to the same place to read or post messages.

And Now the News(group)

The Internet equivalent of the bulletin board is the Usenet newsgroup. Begun in 1979, today Usenet is a worldwide network of approximately 4,000 newsgroups. Usenet messages are copied only once for each ISP supporting the newsgroup. If there are a thousand students on your campus reading the same newsgroup message, there need only be one copy of the message stored on your school's computer.

Newsgroups are categorized by topics, with topics broken down nto subtopics and sub-subtopics. For example, you'll find newsgroups devoted to computers, hobbies, science, social issues, and "alternatives." Newsgroups in this last category cover a wide range of topics that may not appeal to the mainstream. Also in this category are beginning newsgroups.

Usenet names are amalgams of their topics and subtopics, separated by dots. If you were interested in a newsgroup dealing with, say, music, you might start with rec.music and move down to rec.music.radiohead, or rec.music.techno, and so forth. The naming scheme allows you to zero in on a topic of interest.

Getting into the News(group) Business

Most of the work of reading, responding to, and posting messages is handled by a news reader client program, accessible through both Netscape Communicator and Microsoft Internet Explorer. You can not only surf the Web and handle your mail via your browser, but also drop into your favorite newsgroups virtually all in one operation. For a searchable list of newsgroups, see www.liszt.com/news.

To reach newsgroups via Netscape Communicator, go to the Communicator menu bar and select **Newsgroups.** Then, from the File menu, select **Subscribe.** A dialogue box will open that displays a list of available groups. To subscribe to a newsgroup—that is, to tell your news reader you want to be kept up-to-date on the messages posted to a particular group—highlight the group of interest and click on **Subscribe.** Alternately, you can click in the Subscribe column to the right of the group name. The check mark in the Subscribe column means you're "in." Now, click **OK.**

The message center in Netscape Communicator displays a list of newsgroups on your subscription list. Double click on the one of current interest, and your reader presents you with a list of messages posted on the group's bulletin board. Double click on a message to open its contents in a window.

Often, messages contain "Re:" in their subject lines, indicating a response to a previous message (the letters stand for "Regarding"). Many news readers maintain *threads* for you. Threads are chains of messages and all responses to that message. These readers give you the option to read messages chronologically or to read a message followed by its responses.

When you subscribe to a newsgroup, your news reader will also keep track of the messages you've read so that it can present you with the newest (unread) ones. While older messages are still available to you, this feature guarantees that you stay up-to-date without any record keeping on your part. Subscribing to a newsgroup is free, and the subscription information resides on your computer. Newsgroups have no way of knowing who their subscribers are, and the same caveat that applies to bookmarks applies to newsgroups. Information about your subscriptions resides physically on the personal computer you're using. If you switch computers, as in a lab, your subscription information and history of read messages are beyond your reach.

part
1

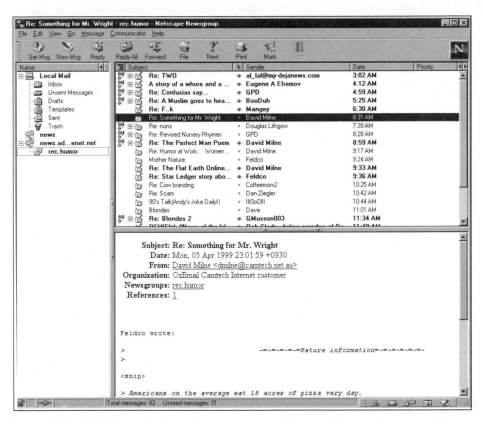

The top part of this figure shows a listing of posted messages. While not visible from this black and white reproduction, a red indicator in the Subject column marks unread messages. Double-clicking on a message opens its contents into a window shown in the bottom part of this figure. You can reply to this message via the Reply icon, or get the next message using the Next icon.

Welcome to the Internet, Miss Manners

While we're on the subject of Internet communication, here are some *netiquette* (net etiquette) tips.

Email Tips. When you send email to someone, even someone who knows you well, all they have to look at are your words—there's no body language attached. That means there's no smile, no twinkle in the eye, no raised eyebrow; and especially, there's no tone of voice. What you write is open to interpretation. You may understand the context of a remark, but will your reader?

If you have any doubts about how your message will be interpreted, you might want to tack an *emoticon* onto your message. An emoticon is a face created out of keyboard characters. For example, there's the happy Smiley :-) (you have to look at it sideways . . . the parenthesis is its mouth), the frowning Smiley :-((Frownie?), the winking Smiley ;-), and so forth. Smileys are the body language of the Internet. Use them to put remarks into context. "Great" in response to a friend's suggestion means you like the idea. "Great :-(" changes the meaning to one of disappointment or sarcasm. (Want a complete list of emoticons? Try using "emoticon" as a keyword for a Web search.)

Keep email messages on target. One of the benefits of email is its speed. Reading through lengthy messages leaves the reader wondering when you'll get to the point. Use short subject headings to indicate what the message is about.

Email's speed carries with it a certain responsibility. Its ease of use encourages quick responses, but quick doesn't necessarily mean thoughtful. Once you hit the **Send** icon, that message is gone. There's no recall button. Think before you write, lest you feel the wrath of the modern-day version of your parents' adage: Answer in haste, repent at leisure.

part

1

Listserv Tips. New listserv subscribers customarily wait a while before joining the discussion. After all, you're electronically strolling into a room full of strangers; it's only fair to see what topics are being discussed before wading in with your own opinions. Otherwise, you're like the bore at the party who elbows his way into a conversation with "But enough about you, let's talk about me." You'll also want to avoid the faux pas of posting a long missive on a topic that subscribers spent the preceding three weeks thrashing out.

Observe the list for a while. Understand its tone and feel, what topics are of interest to others and what areas are taboo. Also, look for personalities. Who's the most vociferous? Who writes very little but responds thoughtfully? Who's the most flexible? The most rigid?

Most of all, keep in mind that there are far more observers than participants. What you write may be read by 10 or 100 times more people than those whose names show up in the daily messages. Do not clutter up the list with "me, too" messages, or quote entire previous messages (only the part to which you're referring). Remember that messages arrive in the email box of subscribers and can fill it up.

Newsgroup Tips. Hang out for a while, or *lurk,* to familiarize yourself with the style, tone, and content of newsgroup messages. As you probably surmised from the names of the groups, their topics of discussion are quite narrow. One of the no-no's of newsgroups is posting messages on subjects outside the focus of the group. Posting off-topic messages, especially lengthy ones, is an excellent way to attract flaming.

A *flame* is a brutally debasing message from one user to another. Flames are designed to hurt and offend, and often the target of the flame feels compelled to respond in kind to protect his or her self-esteem. This leads to a *flame war,* as other users take sides and set flames of their own. If you find yourself the target of a flame, your best strategy is to ignore it. As with a campfire, if no one tends to the flames, they soon die out.

Keep your messages short and to the point. Many newsgroup visitors connect to the Internet via modems. Downloading a day's worth of long postings, especially uninteresting ones, is annoying and frustrating. Similarly, don't post the same message to multiple, related newsgroups. This is called *cross posting,* and it's a peeve of Net citizens who check into these groups. If you've ever flipped the television from channel to channel during a commercial break only to encounter the same commercial (an advertising practice called *roadblocking*), you can imagine how annoying it is to drop in on several newsgroups only to find the same messages posted to each one.

With the huge potential audience newsgroups offer, you might think you've found an excellent medium for advertising goods or services. After all, posting a few messages appears analogous to running classified ads in newspapers, only here the cost is free. There's a name for these kinds of messages—*spam*. Spam is the junk mail of the Internet, and the practice of spamming is a surefire way to attract flames. The best advice for handling spam? Don't answer it. Not only does an answer encourage the spammer, but he or she will also undoubtedly put your email address on a list and sell it to other spammers, who will flood your online mailbox with their junk.

Above all, be considerate of others. Treat them the way you'd like to be treated. Do you enjoy having your grammar or word choices corrected in front of the whole world? Do you feel comfortable when someone calls you stupid in public? Do you appreciate having your religion, ethnicity, heritage, or gender belittled in front of an audience? Respect the rights and feelings of others, if not out of simple decency, then out of the sanctions your ISP may impose. Although you have every right to express an unpopular opinion or to take issue with the postings

part

1

of others, most ISPs have regulations about the kinds of messages one can send via their facilities. Obscenities, threats, and spam may, at a minimum, result in your losing Internet access privileges.

Let's Chat

Virtual chatrooms let you communicate with others around the world in real time by typing on your keyboard. Unless moderated, chats tend to be rather chaotic, with comments going by fast and more than one conversation taking place at the same time!

When arriving in a chatroom, it's customary to say "hi" to whomever's there. Once you type a message, press Enter to send it. Since there may be a lag time between what you say and the answer, wait a few minutes. Do not type in all caps; this is SHOUTING. Describe your actions to make communication clearer (e.g., pounds on table for emphasis).

Types of chat programs include:

- *Web-based chat programs.* Web sites sometimes include a chatroom on a specific subject. Excite, AltaVista, and Yahoo all have free chatrooms. Look for a list of scheduled chats and topics.

- *Internet Relay Chat (IRC).* This method requires using special commands. An IRC server has chatrooms called "channels" where people talk, using nicknames. To use IRC, you need special software such as mIRC, a free program for the PC. You can download this program plus get instructions at the mIRC Homepage (www.geocities.com/~mirc).

- *ICQ.* ICQ ("I Seek You") began in 1997. ICQ networks contain lists of chatrooms. ICQ also lets you know when friends log on so that you can chat with them while still surfing the Internet. For this to work, both you and your friends must be using ICQ. See the official ICQ site at web.icq.com.

Netscape Instant Messenger is similar to chat in that communication occurs in real time. It is different in that messages are private, sent to an individual on a Buddy List that you create.

Virtual worlds, with either a social or educational function, also allow real-time chat. A *MUD (Multi-User Dimension)* or *MOO (Multi-user Object Oriented)* is a type of text-based virtual reality. It contains a narrative description of places, buildings, rooms, objects within rooms, and characters. You use special commands to chat with others, interact with objects, or create your own rooms and objects (with permission). Most MOOs or MUDs must be accessed through Telnet or a client program such as Tiny Fugue (tf.tcp.com/~hawkeye/tf/). Diversity University, an educational MOO, provides access through a Web Gateway located at http://moo.dumain.du.org:8000/, which makes it possible to see pictures.

Avatar virtual worlds contain two- or three-dimensional visual representations of a place. You choose a visual character called an "avatar" to represent yourself. You can chat with others or explore the world with special keys on your keyboard that allow you to walk, run, or fly! You must download special software to enter a virtual world. One example is ActiveWorlds at www.activeworlds.com. Try their free software, login as a visitor, and choose a world from the menu to visit.

Quick Check

Let's review the types of communication on the Internet:

- Email lets you send and receive letters electronically.
- A listserv lets you send email to a group of subscribers, and receive messages from anyone in that group.
- A newsgroup is like a bulletin board on which messages can be written and responded to by anyone at any time.
- Chat occurs in real time in a virtual chatroom.
- MUDs and MOOs are virtual text-based worlds. Avatar worlds have graphical representations of places and characters.

part

1

Security Issues

How Not to Come Down with a Virus

Downloading files from the Internet allows less responsible Net citizens to unleash onto your computer viruses, worms, and Trojan horses, all dangerous programs that fool you into thinking they're doing one thing while they're actually erasing your hard disk or performing some other undesirable task. Protection is your responsibility.

One way to reduce the risk of contracting a virus is to download software from reliable sites. Corporations such as Microsoft and Apple take care to make sure downloadable software is virus free. So do most institutions that provide software downloads as a public service (such as the Stanford University archives of Macintosh software). Be especially careful with programs you find on someone's home page. If you're not sure about safe download sources, ask around in a newsgroup, talk to friends, or check with the information technology center on campus.

In addition, be careful about downloading suspicious-looking email attachments, especially from someone you don't know. Even if you know the person the message appears to be from, someone could have obtained their email address and used it to send you a virus. If the subject heading sounds strange, it's better to ask questions now than to download and be sorry later!

You can also buy and use a reliable virus program. Symantec and Dr. Solomon sell first-rate programs for the Mac and PC. You can update these programs right from the Internet so they'll detect the most current viruses. Most of the time, these programs can disinfect files/documents on your hard drive that contain viruses. Don't forget to check files on your diskettes as well.

Crude as it may sound, downloading programs from the Internet without using a virus check is like having unprotected sex with a stranger. While downloading software may not be life-threatening, imagine the consequences if your entire hard disk, including all your course work and software, is totally obliterated. It won't leave you feeling very good.

Keeping Things to Yourself

The Internet is not private. Information you pass around the Internet is stored on, or passed along by, computers that are accessible to others. Your ISP may provide member directories that list all subscribers and their addresses. Your activities at a Web site can be tracked, including which pages you visited. Cookies, files left on your hard drive by certain sites, make it easy for advertisers to find out your interests.

Just as you take care to protect your wallet or purse while walking down a crowded street, it's also a good practice to exercise caution with information you'd like to keep (relatively) private. Although computer system administrators take great care to ensure the security of this information, no scheme is completely infallible. Here are some security tips:

- Exercise care when sending sensitive information such as credit card numbers, social security numbers, passwords, even telephone num-

part

1

bers and addresses in email. Your email message may pass through four or five computers en route to its destination, and at any of these points, it can be intercepted and read by someone other than the recipient.

■ Send personal information over the Web only if the page is secure. Web browsers automatically encrypt information on secure pages, and the information can only be unscrambled at the Web site that created the secure page. In Netscape Communicator, a lock with a yellow glow around it, appearing above the option "Security" in the menu bar, indicates a secure web page. Click on Security to read more information about the page. In Microsoft Internet Explorer, a key at the bottom right corner of the screen indicates a secure site.

■ Remember that any files you store on your ISP's computer are accessible to unscrupulous hackers. See if your ISP has a privacy policy, and find out what it says. Consider whether you really want to post a "member profile" with information about yourself.

■ Protect your password. Many Web client programs, such as mail clients, maintain your password for you. That means anyone with physical access to your computer can read your email. With a few simple tools, someone can even steal your password. Never leave your password on a lab computer. (Make sure the **Remember Password** or **Save Password** box is unchecked in any application that asks for your password.) It helps to change your password often and use a combination of letters and numbers meaningful only to you.

■ If shopping online, check for contact information such as a phone number. Ask others about the vendor's reputation. Do not click on links in email sent by advertisers (they're probably checking to see if your email address is active). Consider getting a separate email account from a free provider such as Excite or Onebox.com and using it for shopping.

■ The contents of any message you post become public information, but in a newsgroup your email address also becomes public knowledge. Use common sense about posting information you or someone else expects to remain private. Many newsgroup postings are archived (stored for a long period of time) and can be searched by search engines.

part

1

Finally, remember that the Web in particular and the Internet in general are communications media with a far-reaching audience, and placing information on the Internet is tantamount to publishing it. Information can and will be read by people with different tastes and sensitivities. The Web tends to be self-censoring, so be prepared to handle feedback, both good and bad.

Using the Internet for Research: Critical Evaluation

Much of your time online will be spent on researching your chosen field. Typical research resources, such as journal articles, books, and other scholarly works, are reviewed by a panel of experts before being published. At the very least, any reputable publisher takes care to assure that the author is who he or she claims to be and that the work being published represents an informed point of view. When anyone can post anything in a Web site or to a newsgroup, the burden of assessing the relevance and accuracy of what you read falls to you. Rumors quickly grow into facts on the Internet simply because stories spread so rapidly that the "news" seems to be everywhere. Because the Internet leaves few tracks, in no time it's impossible to tell whether you are reading independent stories or the same story that's been around the world two or three times. Gathering information on the Internet may be quick, but verifying the quality of information requires a serious commitment.

Approach researching via the Internet with confidence, however, not trepidation. You'll find it an excellent workout for your critical evaluation skills. No matter what career you pursue, employers value an employee who can think critically and independently. Critical thinking is also the basis of problem solving, another ability highly valued. So, as you research your academic projects, be assured that you're simultaneously developing lifelong expertise.

The first tip for successful researching on the Internet is to always consider your source. A Web site's URL often alerts you to the sponsor of the site. CNN or MSNBC are established news organizations, and you can give the information you find at their sites the same weight you would give to their cablecasts. Likewise, major newspapers operate Web sites with articles reprinted from their daily editions or expanded stories written expressly for the Internet. On the other hand, if you're unfamiliar with the source, treat the information the way you would any new data. Look for specifics—"66 percent of all voters" as opposed to "most voters"—and for information that can be verified, such as a cited report in another medium or information accessible through a Web site hosted by a credible sponsor.

Look for independent paths to the same information. This can involve careful use of search engines or visits to newsgroups with both similar and opposing viewpoints. Make sure that the "independent" information you find is truly independent. In newsgroups, don't discount the possibility of multiple postings, or that a posting in one group is nothing more than a quotation from a posting in another. Ways to verify independent paths include following sources (if any) back to their origins, contacting the person who posted a message and asking for clarification, or checking other media for verification.

In many cases, you can use your common sense to raise your comfort level about the soundness of the information. With both listservs and newsgroups, it's possible to lurk for a while to develop a feeling for the authors of various postings. Who seems the most authoritarian, and who seems to be "speaking" from emotion or bias? Who seems to know what he or she is talking about on a regular basis? Do these people cite their sources of information (a job or affiliation perhaps)? Do they have a history of thoughtful, insightful postings, or do their postings typically contain generalities, unjustifiable claims, or flames? On Web sites, where the information feels more anonymous, there are also clues you can use to test for authenticity. Verify who's hosting the Web site. If the host or domain name is unfamiliar to you, perhaps a search engine can help you locate more information. Measure the tone and style of the writing at the site. Does it seem consistent with the education level and knowledge base necessary to write intelligently about the subject?

When offering an unorthodox point of view, good authors supply facts, figures, and quotes to buttress their positions, expecting readers to be skeptical of their claims. Knowledgeable authors on the Internet follow these same commonsense guidelines. Be suspicious of authors who expect you to agree with their points of view simply because they've published them on the Internet. In one-on-one encounters, you frequently judge the authority and knowledge of the speaker using criteria you'd be hard-pressed to explain. Use your sense of intuition on the Internet, too.

As a researcher (and as a human being), the job of critical thinking requires a combination of healthy skepticism and rabid curiosity. Newsgroups and Web sites tend to focus narrowly on single issues (newsgroups more so than Web sites). Don't expect to find a torrent of opposing views on newsgroup postings; their very nature and reason for existence dampens free-ranging discussions. A newsgroup on *The X-Files* might argue about whether extraterrestrials exist, but not about whether the program is the premier television show on the air today. Such a discussion would

part

1

run counter to the purposes of the newsgroup. Anyone posting such a message would be flamed, embarrassed, ignored, or otherwise driven away.

It's Okay to Be Critical

Your research responsibilities include searching for opposing views by visiting a variety of newsgroups and Web sites. It helps here to fall back on the familiar questions of journalism: who, what, when, where, and why.

Who else might speak knowledgeably on this subject? Enter that person's name into a search engine. You might be surprised to find whose work is represented on the Web. (For fun, one of the authors entered the name of a rock-and-roll New York radio disk jockey into MetaCrawler and was amazed to find several pages devoted to the DJ, including sound clips of broadcasts dating back to the 1960s, along with a history of his theme song.)

What event might shed more information on your topic? Is there a group or organization that represents your topic? Do they hold an annual conference? Are synopses of presentations posted on the sponsoring organization's Web site?

When do events happen? Annual meetings or seasonal occurrences can help you isolate newsgroup postings of interest.

Where might you find this information? If you're searching for information on wines, for example, check to see if major wine-producing regions, such as the Napa Valley in California or the Rhine Valley in Germany, sponsor Web sites. These may point you to organizations or information not found in other searches. Remember, Web search engines are fallible; they don't find every site you need.

Why is the information you're searching for important? The answer to this question can lead you to related fields. New drugs, for example, are important not only to victims of diseases but to drug companies and the Food and Drug Administration as well.

Approach assertions from a skeptic's point of view. See if they stand up to critical evaluation or if you're merely emotionally attached to them. Imagine "What if . . . ?" or "What about . . . ?" scenarios that may disprove or at least call into question what you're reading. Try following each assertion you pull from the Internet with the phrase "on the other hand. . . ." Because you can't leave the sentence hanging, you'll be

part

1

forced to finish it, and this will help get you into the habit of critically examining information.

These are, of course, the same techniques critical thinkers have employed for centuries, only now you are equipped with more powerful search tools than past researchers may have ever imagined. In the time it took them to formulate questions, you can search dozens of potential information sources. You belong to the first generation of college students to enjoy both quantity and quality in your research, along with a wider perspective on issues and the ability to form opinions after reasoning from a much wider knowledge base.

Certainly, the potential exists for the Internet to grind out a generation of intellectual robots who regurgitate information from many sources. Technology has always had its good and bad aspects; however, computer communications technology provides us the potential to become some of the best-informed thinkers in the history of the world. Aided by this technology, we may become thinkers who are not only articulate, but confident that our opinions have been distilled from a range of views and processed by our own personalities, beliefs, and biases. This is one of the aspects of the Internet that makes this era such an exciting combination of humanism and technology.

part

1

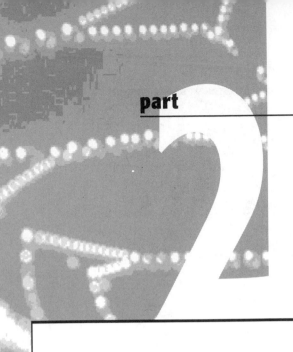

Internet Resources for Educators of Students with Exceptionalities

Part 2 of this guide contains information designed to help teachers and prospective teachers use the Internet and the World Wide Web in their work with students with exceptionalities. My intention is to provide basic information needed by special and general educators as well as useful and interesting resources. The Web sites in this guide have been selected to be representative of the best the Web has to offer. For the most part, national organizations and comprehensive Web sites are highlighted rather than isolated local or regional pages, although occasionally I have included a site simply because of the interesting or hard-to-find information it provides. I have tried to stay away from sites that were created purely for the purpose of selling a product or a particular agenda. My hope is that this information will expand your knowledge base, enrich your teaching, and help you discover the possibilities of the Web.

Why Are the Internet and the World Wide Web Important for Special Education?

A major advantage of the Internet is that it provides a connection to other people. In addition to email, the Internet provides an opportunity to use chat rooms and newsgroups to talk to and ask questions of all stakeholders (people who are disabled, parents, and professionals) in the education of students with disabilities. We Media is a great place to

start. Similar to Yahoo, Excite, and other Internet portals, it is an integrated online community created by and for people with disabilities, their families and friends.

We Media: The Disability Network

http://www.wemedia.com

There are many resources on various disabilities/syndromes that previously would have been difficult, if not impossible to locate. For example, where could you find information if someone asked you about hyperlexia, Rett syndrome, Angelman syndrome, or Williams syndrome? Chances are that you wouldn't be able to find the information by pulling a book off the shelf or even spending hours in the library. However, with a few clicks of the mouse, not only can you find in-depth information on the characteristics, identification, and treatment of various disabilities, but you can also link to support groups for families.

American Hyperlexia Association

http://www.hyperlexia.org

Rett Syndrome

http://www.isn.net/~jypsy/rett.htm

Angelman Syndrome Foundation

http://www.angelman.org

Williams Syndrome Association

http://www.williams-syndrome.org

There are many library resources available on the Internet. University libraries frequently provide enrolled students access to the full text of scholarly articles on line. Visit your university's Web site and see what it has to offer.

Other Web sites contain databases that enable you to find scholarly articles, as well as updates on the latest research and promising practices. For example, the ERIC (Educational Resources Information Center) system is a nationwide information network of 16 federally funded clearinghouses. The ERIC Clearinghouse on Disabilities and Gifted

part

2

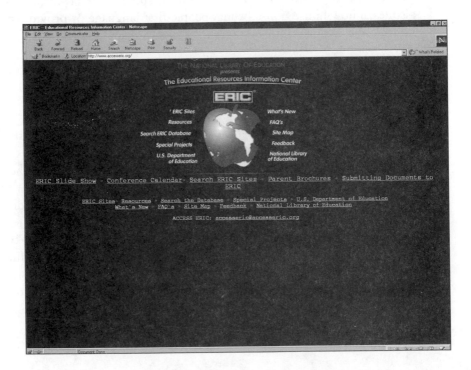

Education (ERIC EC) gathers and disseminates professional literature, information, and resources via databases, fact sheets, frequently asked questions (FAQs), and mini-bibliographies. The ERIC EC database contains more than 70,000 citations on disabilities or gifted topics.

The Educational Resources Information Center

http://www.accesseric.org

ERIC Clearinghouse on Disabilities and Gifted Education

http://ericec.org

The Internet as a Tool for Your Studies in Special Education

Using the Internet, you can expand your knowledge base about the historical context and legal basis for special education. You can obtain information on current laws, regulations, and court cases that enable the teacher to understand both the letter and the spirit of the law. You can also learn how to use non-labeling, people-first language or provide this information to others.

HISTORICAL AND PHILOSOPHICAL BACKGROUND OF SPECIAL EDUCATION

Special Education as an Outgrowth of the Civil Rights Movement   Historically, people with disabilities have been excluded from society. The biggest advances in civil rights came as an outgrowth of the civil rights movements of the 1960s. As African Americans, women, and other social minorities gained political influence, so, too, did people with disabilities. Public Law 94-142, the first comprehensive federal special education law, was passed in 1975. However, it was not until 1990 and the passage of the Americans with Disabilities Act, which contains wording similar to the Civil Rights Act of 1964 and Section 504 of the Vocational Rehabilitation Act of 1973, that people with disabilities won the legal right to freedom from discrimination.

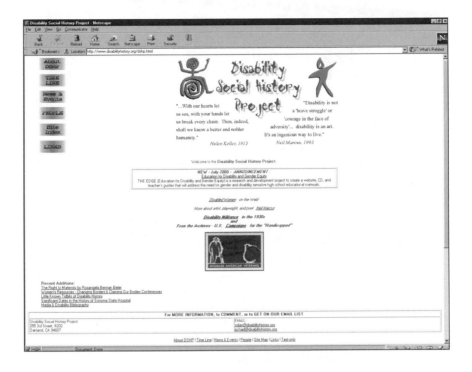

Disability Social History Project

http://www.disabilityhistory.org/dshp.html

A timeline provides significant dates and other important information about the history of people with disabilities and special education.

Non-Labeling Language   The language we use when referring to people with disabilities can either convey respect and dignity, or it can demean or dishonor them. Special educators should avoid using language that has negative connotations and evokes pity or fear. Learn why language can make a difference and how to use it appropriately.

Disability Etiquette Handbook

http://www.ci.sat.tx.us/planning/handbook

People First Language

http://www.kidstogether.org/pep-1st.htm

The Utterly Adaptable Etiquette Guide

```
http://www.labor.state.ut.us/
Utah_Antidiscrimination__Labo/defdis/etiquett/
etiquett.htm
```

Words with Dignity

```
http://www.paraquad.org/wwd.htm
```

Special Education Terminology   Help in understanding special education terminology can be found at the following Web sites.

Alphabet Soup: Disability Related Acronyms

```
http://www.disabilityresources.org/ABC.html
```

Confused by the alphabet soup of disability-related terms on documents and reports? Here's a quick guide to some of the more common acronyms in disability education, law, medicine, and rehabilitation.

Glossary of Special Ed Terms

```
http://www.disabilityrights.org/glossary.htm
```

The Special Educator as Advocate   In its Code of Ethics and Standards of Practice, The Council for Exceptional Children has clearly stated that educators should "serve as advocates for exceptional students by speaking, writing, and acting in a variety of situations on their behalf."

Code of Ethics and Standards of Practice for Educators of Persons with Exceptionalities

```
http://www.cec.sped.org/ps/code.htm
```

The following Web sites provide information for people interested in working for the rights of people with disabilities.

The Disability Rights Activist

```
http://disrights.org
```

Disability Rights Education and Defense Fund (DREDF)

`http://www.dredf.org`

DREDF is a national law and policy center dedicated to protecting and advancing the civil rights of people with disabilities through legislation, litigation, advocacy, technical assistance, and education and training of attorneys, advocates, persons with disabilities, and parents of children with disabilities.

The National Association of Protection and Advocacy Systems

`http://protectionandadvocacy.com`

Wrightslaw: The Special Ed Advocate

`http://www.wrightslaw.com`

Subscribe to The Special Ed Advocate, a free online newsletter about special ed law, advocacy, research, and other topics.

LEGAL ASPECTS OF EDUCATING STUDENTS WITH EXCEPTIONALITIES

The Individuals with Disabilities Education Act (IDEA)   The IDEA is the federal special education law. Originally passed in 1975 as the Education of All Handicapped Children Act (P.L.94-142), the 1997 Amendments and the federal regulations that implement the law are available on many Web sites. One of the most comprehensive sites, Idea Practices, answers your questions about the Individuals with Disabilities Education Act. It contains a hyper-linked version of the federal regulations by section and subject area as well as Department of Education updates, the annual report to Congress on implementation of the IDEA, and other law-related resources. Resources include strategies and teaching methods for specific disabilities and situations, as well as case studies from schools implementing promising practices.

Idea Practices

http://www.ideapractices.org

part

2

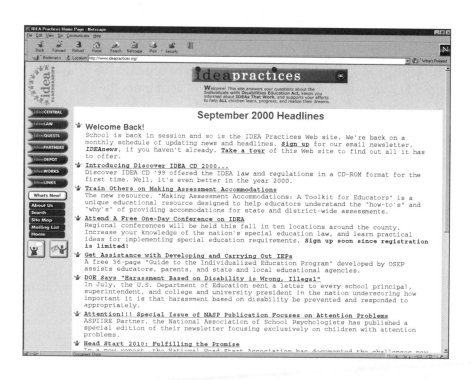

IDEA '97

`http://www.ed.gov/offices/OSERS/IDEA/index.html`

Section 504 of the Vocational Rehabilitation Act   Section 504 prohibits discrimination on the basis of disability in federally funded programs. In schools that receive any kind of federal funding, all students with disabilities are entitled to reasonable accommodations under Section 504, whether or not they receive special education services.

Federal Requirements for Free Appropriate Public Education under Section 504

`http://www.ed.gov/offices/OCR/fape.html`

Section 504 and Education

`http://www.ed.gov/offices/OCR/ocr504.html`

The Americans with Disabilities Act (ADA)   The ADA is wide ranging legislation that prohibits discrimination against people with disabilities in the areas of employment, public services and accommodations, and telecommunications. It is intended to make American society more accessible for people with disabilities.

part

2

Americans with Disabilities Act Document Center

`http://janweb.icdi.wvu.edu/kinder/index.htm`

U.S. Department of Justice ADA Home Page

`http://www.usdoj.gov/crt/ada/adahom1.htm`

Do you have trouble understanding the basic provisions of these laws? Wondering how to explain them to parents or other teachers? The following Web sites provide comparisons among the three laws:

Section 504 and IDEA: Basic Similarities and Differences

`http://www.edlaw.net/service/504idea.html`

Comparative Analysis: IDEA, Section 504 and the ADA

`http://at-advocacy.phillynews.com/misc/cohen2.html`

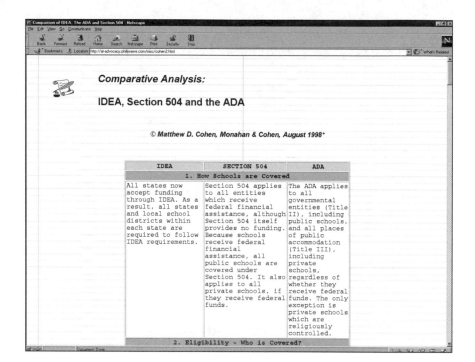

Government   The U.S. Department of Education's Office of Special Education and Rehabilitative Services (OSERS) is the branch of the government that supports special education programs for individuals from birth through 21, provides rehabilitation of youth and adults with disabilities, and supports research.

Office of Special Education and Rehabilitative Services

`http://www.ed.gov/offices/OSERS`

The OSERS Web site links to each of its three branches:

Office of Special Education Programs

`http://www.ed.gov/offices/OSERS/OSEP/index.html`

The Office of Special Education Programs is responsible for administering programs and projects relating to the free appropriate public education of all children, youth and adults with disabilities, from birth through age 21. The Web site for this agency contains the latest news regarding special education programs and many resources for teachers, including training materials related to the IDEA, copies of reports on

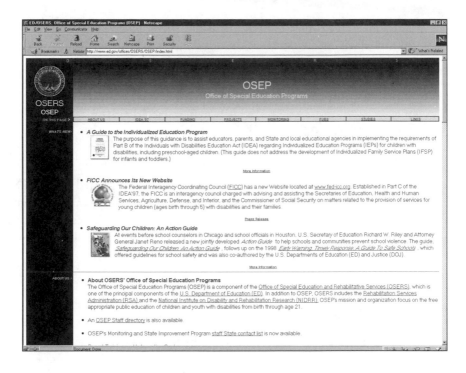

part

2

topics such as preventing school violence, funding information, and a searchable database of projects.

The Rehabilitation Services Administration

`http://www.ed.gov/offices/OSERS/RSA/index.html`

The Rehabilitation Services Administration develops and implements comprehensive and coordinated programs of vocational rehabilitation, supported employment, and independent living for individuals with disabilities, through services, training, research and economic opportunities, in order to maximize their employability, independence, and integration into the workplace and the community.

The National Institute on Disability and Rehabilitation Research

`http://www.ed.gov/offices/OSERS/NIDRR`

The National Institute on Disability and Rehabilitation Research conducts comprehensive and coordinated programs of research and related activities to maximize the full inclusion, social integration, employment, and independent living of disabled individuals of all ages.

The Supreme Court   Information about special education and the Supreme Court can be found at the following Web sites.

The Oyez Project

`http://oyez.nwu.edu`

The Oyez Project is a collection of multimedia files related to the U.S. Supreme Court. You can hear streaming audio clips of oral arguments and read written opinions from many Supreme Court cases. The site also features a virtual tour of the Supreme Court building and biographies and photos of justices.

The Cornell University Law Library

`http://supct.law.cornell.edu/supct`

The Supreme Court Collection from the Legal Information Institute at Cornell University.

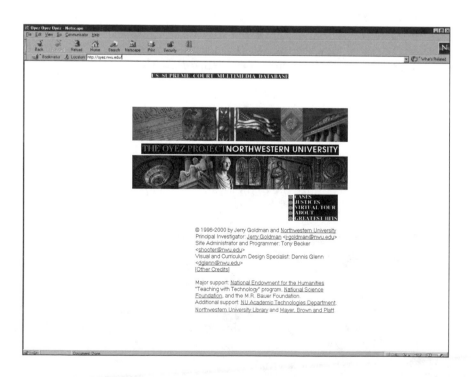

DOCUMENTING ELECTRONIC SOURCES IN YOUR SCHOLARLY WRITING

The American Psychological Association's (APA) style of writing is the preferred format for educators in the field of special education. You can find online assistance in writing papers for coursework or submission for publication.

APA Style Resources

`http://www.psychwww.com/resource/apacrib.htm`

Electronic Reference Formats Recommended by the APA

`http://www.apa.org/journals/webref.html`

The American Psychological Association (APA) has created a Web site to assist authors in documenting online sources. The APA approved this extension of the APA manual in 1999.

part
2

A Guide for Writing Research Papers Based on Styles Recommended by The APA

`http://webster.commnet.edu/apa/apa_index.htm`

INFORMATION ON SPECIFIC DISABILITIES UNDER FEDERAL SPECIAL EDUCATION LAW

In order for students to receive special education services under the Individuals with Disabilities Education Act, a multidisciplinary team must determine that they have at least one of the following disabilities and that they need specially designed instruction. First, though, visit a "super site" which contains information on many categories of disability as well as specific resources for parent, teachers, and information on topics such as inclusion, transition, and products for people with disabilities, their families and teachers.

Special Education Resources on the Internet (SERI)

`http://www.hood.edu/seri`

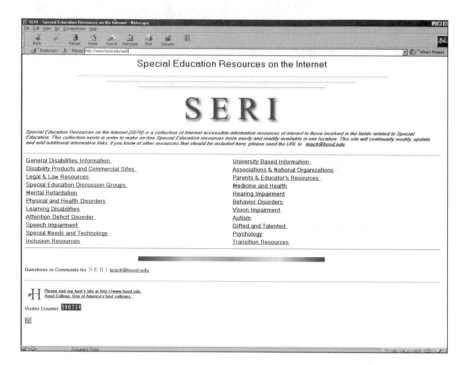

The following sections provide resource information on the categories of disability under the IDEA. For each category, a summary of the federal definition under the IDEA (Section 300.7, Child with a Disability) is provided.

Autism Autism is a developmental disability that significantly affects verbal and nonverbal communication and social interaction. Characteristics often associated with autism are engagement in repetitive activities and stereotyped movements, resistance to environmental change or change in daily routines, and unusual responses to sensory experiences.

Autism Research Institute (ARI)

http://www.autism.com/ari

ARI is primarily devoted to conducting research, and to disseminating the results of research to parents and professionals, on the causes of autism and methods of preventing, diagnosing and treating autism.

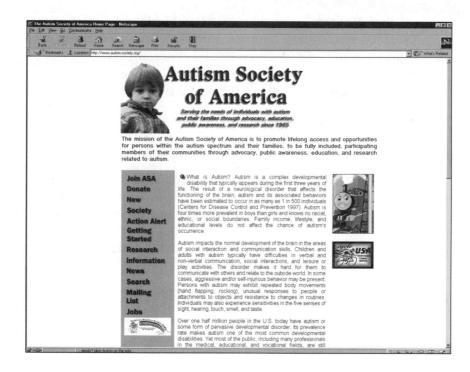

Autism Society of America (ASA)

`http://www.autism-society.org`

The ASA provides information and resources for professionals and families of individuals with autism. The "Getting Started" section provides basic information on autism and treatment approaches.

Center for the Study of Autism

`http://www.autism.org`

Subgroups, issues, interventions, overview in different languages.

Oops. . . . Wrong Planet Syndrome

`http://www.isn.net/~jypsy/index.html`

The mother of a boy with autism created this site. It contains definitions of autism and related disorders and an extensive list of resources and links to other sites ("more links than you can shake a stick at"), as well as mail lists, forums, chat rooms, and newsgroups.

Deaf–Blindness   A student with deaf–blindness has both hearing and visual impairments, the combination of which causes such severe communication and other developmental and educational needs that they cannot be accommodated in special education programs solely for children with deafness or children with blindness.

A–Z to Deaf–Blindness

`http://www.deafblind.com`

This site, created by a man who is deaf and blind, contains information about deaf–blindness, including the deaf–blind manual alphabet. Did you know that a person with a red and white cane is deaf–blind?

D-B Link: National Information Clearinghouse for Children who are Deaf–Blind

`http://www.tr.wou.edu/dblink/index.htm`

Databases, publications, many useful links.

part

2

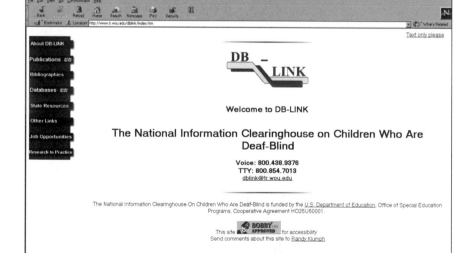

Helen Keller National Center for Deaf-Blind Youths and Adults

`http://www.helenkeller.org/national/index.htm`

Comprehensive information on vocational and personal adjustment training, links to resources and technical assistance to educators.

Deafness   Deafness means a hearing impairment that is so severe that the child is impaired in processing linguistic information through hearing, with or without amplification.

Alexander Graham Bell Association for the Deaf (AGBell)

`http://www.agbell.org`

The Alexander Graham Bell Association for the Deaf and Hard of Hearing (AG Bell) is an international organization comprised of parents, adults with hearing loss, and professionals who serve children with hearing loss. AG Bell was founded in 1890 by Alexander Graham Bell as an information provider and support network. AG Bell is the largest

part

2

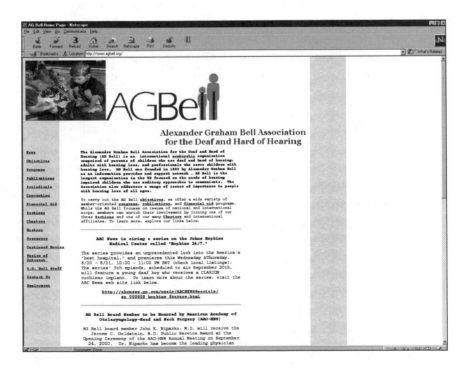

organization in the U.S. focused on the needs of hearing impaired children who use auditory approaches to communicate.

Council on Education of the Deaf

`http://www.educ.kent.edu/deafed`

Curriculum materials, instructional strategies, job board, teacher preparation programs.

The Deaf Education Option Web

`http://www2.pair.com/options`

This site helps families of children with newly diagnosed deafness or hearing impairments decide how to communicate with their children. It offers information on communication methodologies, assistive technology, and frequently asked questions.

part
2

Wallace Library Guides

`http://wally.rit.edu/internet/subject/deafness.html`

Links to an extensive set of resources for people who are deaf or hard of hearing, including several interactive Web-based American Sign Language and fingerspelling sites.

Emotional Disturbance   A student with emotional disturbance exhibits one or more of the following characteristics over a long period of time and to a marked degree:

■ An inability to learn that cannot be explained by intellectual, sensory, or health factors;

■ An inability to build or maintain satisfactory interpersonal relationships with peers and teachers;

■ Inappropriate types of behavior or feelings under normal circumstances;

■ A general pervasive mood of unhappiness or depression

■ A tendency to develop physical symptoms or fears associated with personal or school problems.

The term does not apply to children who are socially maladjusted, or have inappropriate behaviors, unless it is determined that they have an emotional disturbance.

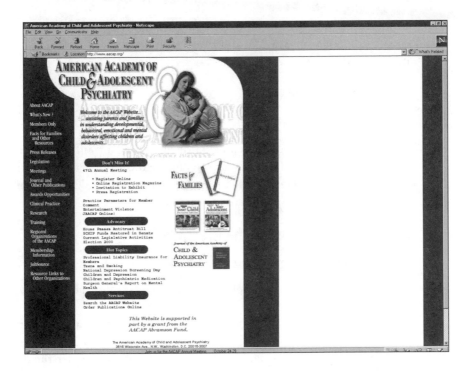

part
2

American Academy of Child and Adolescent Psychiatry

`http://www.aacap.org`

The stated purpose of this site is to assist "parents and families in under-standing developmental, behavioral, emotional and mental disorders affecting children and adolescents." Teachers will benefit from its straightforward fact sheets on a variety of topics, as well as information on the nature of child and adolescent psychiatry. The glossary provides information on alcohol and drug abuse, anorexia nervosa, anxiety, atten-tion deficit hyperactivity disorder, bipolar disorder (manic-depression), bulimia nervosa, conduct disorder, depression, obsessive-compulsive dis-order, physical abuse, post-traumatic stress disorder, psychosis, schizo-phrenia, sexual abuse, suicide, and Tourette's syndrome.

Center for Effective Collaboration and Practice (CECP)

`http://cecp.air.org/index.htm`

CECP promotes collaboration among Federal agencies serving children with or at risk of developing emotional disabilities. This site includes Federal Resources, online resources, including articles, reports, monographs, mini-Web sites, statistics and email listservs, and many links to resources on issues of emotional and behavioral problems in children and youth.

Internet Mental Health

http://www.mentalhealth.com

This Web site is a virtual encyclopedia of mental health information. It contains descriptions, diagnosis, treatment, medications, and research for 54 mental disorders; in-depth information about the 72 most commonly prescribed drugs; and, an online magazine.

National Association for the Mentally Ill

http://www.nami.org/medical.htm

News, research, resources, helpline, books, topical information.

Hearing Impairment   Hearing impairment means an impairment in hearing, whether permanent or fluctuating, that adversely affects a child's educational performance but that is not included under the definition of deafness.

Alexander Graham Bell Association for the Deaf and Hard of Hearing

http://www.agbell.org

This organization focuses on the needs of children with hearing impairments who use auditory approaches to communicate.

Hard of Hearing and Deaf Students: A Resource Guide to Support Classroom Teachers

http://www.bced.gov.bc.ca/specialed/hearimpair/
toc.htm

This site, sponsored by the British Columbia Ministry of Education, provides information for teachers on hearing loss, preparing to teach children with hearing impairments, tips on classroom adaptation and communication.

Mental Retardation   Mental retardation means significantly subaverage general intellectual functioning, existing concurrently with deficits in adaptive behavior and manifested during the developmental period.

National Down Syndrome Association

`http://www.ndss.org`

The NDSS Web site bills itself as a comprehensive, online information source about Down syndrome. One very useful feature for college students is a page created just to help students do research on Down syndrome.

National Fragile X Foundation

`http://www.nfxf.org`

Fragile-X Syndrome is the most common form of genetic inherited mental retardation. The foundation provides information, support, consultation and referrals, as well as a newsletter.

The Arc of the United States

`http://thearc.org`

The Arc is a national advocacy organization for people with mental retardation and related disabilities and their families. You can shop on line for informational materials about mental retardation and related developmental disabilities, and many of these materials are free. In addition to many links, this site provides access to information on the Americans

part

2

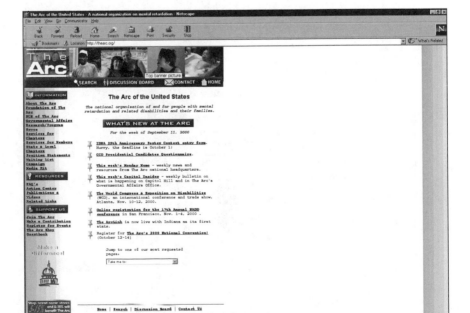

with Disabilities Act, criminal justice, fetal alcohol syndrome, and the human genome project. You can participate in discussions and view the Capitol Insider, a weekly bulletin on what is happening on Capitol Hill.

Multiple Disabilities   Multiple disabilities means impairments that occur at the same time (such as mental retardation-blindness, mental retardation-orthopedic impairment, etc.), the combination of which causes such severe educational needs that they cannot be accommodated in special education programs solely for one of the impairments. The term does not include deaf-blindness.

Activity Ideas for Students with Severe/Profound/ Multiple Disabilities

http://www.palaestra.com/featurestory.html

A feature article by PALAESTRA (Forum of Sport, Physical Education, and Recreation for People with Disabilities) presents six units of activities that could easily be carried out by teachers.

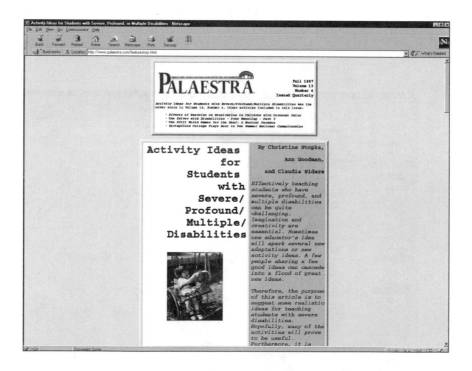

The Association for Persons with Severe Disabilities

http://www.tash.org

Conferences, newsletter, discussion groups, grassroots advocacy.

Orthopedic Impairment   The federal definition of orthopedic impairment merely lists example of disabilities that are considered orthopedic impairments. An orthopedic impairment is a motor disability caused by an anomaly, disease, or other condition (for example, cerebral palsy, spina bifida, muscular dystrophy, or traumatic injury) where the child requires specialized and integrated services in order to benefit from an educational program.

Information about Mobility Impairments

http://spot.pcc.edu/osd/mobinfo.htm

Muscular Dystrophy Association

http://www.mdausa.org

A comprehensive guide to materials about 40 different neuromuscular diseases, plus information about the usual age of onset and characteristics of each disorder.

Strategies for Teaching Children with Motor/Orthopedic Impairments

http://www.as.wvu.edu/~scidis/motor.html

United Cerebral Palsy Association

http://www.ucpa.org

United Cerebral Palsy's mission is to advance the independence, productivity and full citizenship of people with cerebral palsy and other disabilities, through a commitment to independence, inclusion, and self-determination. The Web site provides information on advocacy initiatives, links to national resources and information, and much more.

part

2

Other Health Impairment Including Attention Deficit Disorder   Other health impairment means having limited strength, vitality or alertness, including a heightened alertness to environmental stimuli, that results in limited alertness with respect to the educational environment. The impairment is due to chronic or acute health problems such as asthma, attention deficit disorder or attention deficit hyperactivity disorder, diabetes, epilepsy, a heart condition, hemophilia, lead poisoning, leukemia, nephritis, rheumatic fever, and sickle cell anemia.

Band-aides and Blackboards: When Chronic Illness or Some Other Medical Problem Goes to School

http://funrsc.fairfield.edu/~jfleitas/sitemap.html

Tons of information for children, teens, and adults, including tips for teachers, nurses, doctors, and parents.

Candlelighters' Childhood Cancer Foundation

http://candlelighters.org

Provides support, advocacy, and information for parents affected by pediatric AIDS.

CHADD

http://www.chadd.org

Children and Adults with Attention Deficit Disorder support group and information/resources.

Elizabeth Glaser Pediatric AIDS Foundation

http://www.pedaids.org

A worldwide nonprofit organization dedicated to identifying, funding, and conducting AIDS/HIV research.

The Epilepsy Foundation

http://www.efa.org

The Epilepsy Foundation (formerly the Epilepsy Foundation of America) is a national organization that works for people affected by seizures through research, education, advocacy, and service. A section of this Web site is devoted to information for teachers.

part

2

The Foundation for Medically Fragile Children

http://www.care4gakids.com

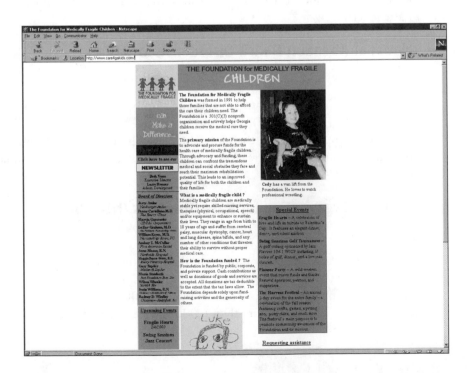

The Foundation is a nonprofit organization providing funds for the health care of children who are medically fragile in the home or out-patient setting.

National Attention Deficit Disorder Association

http://www.add.org

This site is about research, treatment, and family and legal issues pertaining to ADD and ADHD. It features personal stories and has Kid's Area in which children are encouraged to provide their opinions and thoughts about the disorders. Also contains links to support groups and other Web sites.

National Organization for Rare Disorders (NORD)

http://www.rarediseases.org

NORD is a unique federation of more than 140 not-for-profit voluntary health organizations serving people with rare disorders and disabilities. A rare or "orphan" disease affects fewer than 200,000 people in the United States. There are more than 6,000 rare disorders that, taken together, affect approximately 25 million Americans. NORD serves as a clearinghouse for information on rare disorders and provides referrals to additional sources of assistance and ongoing support.

Specific Learning Disability   A learning disability is disorder in one or more of the basic psychological processes involved in understanding or in using spoken or written language that may manifest itself in an imperfect ability to listen, think, speak, read, write, spell, or to do mathematical calculations. It includes conditions such as perceptual disabilities, brain injury, minimal brain dysfunction, dyslexia, and developmental aphasia. The term does not include learning problems that are primarily the result of visual, hearing, or motor disabilities, of mental retardation, of emotional disturbance, or of environmental, cultural, or economic disadvantage.

Dyslexia: The Gift

`http://www.dyslexia.com`

This searchable site with information about dyslexia includes curriculum aids for teachers with students who are dyslexic, a bookstore, a discussion board, and links.

part
2

International Dyslexia Society

`http://www.interdys.org`

The International Dyslexia Association (IDA) (formerly The Orton Dyslexia Society) is an international, 501(c)(3) nonprofit, scientific and educational organization dedicated to the study and treatment of dyslexia.

Internet Special Education Resources

`http://www.iser.com`

Nationwide directory of professionals who serve learning disabilities and special education communities in assessment, placements, therapy, advocacy.

The Learning Disabilities Association of America

`http://www.ldanatl.org`

LDA is a national, nonprofit organization whose purpose is to advance the education and general welfare of children and adults of normal or

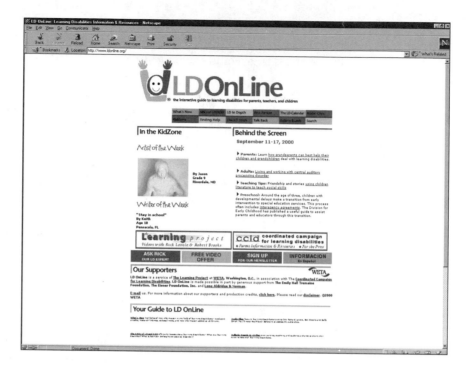

potentially normal intelligence who manifest disabilities of a perceptual, conceptual, or coordinative nature.

LD Online

`http://www.ldonline.org`

This interactive guide to learning disabilities for parents, students, and teachers offers newsletters, teaching tips, and more.

National Center for Learning Disabilities, Inc.

`http://www.ncld.org`

News, links, resources for families and professionals.

Teens Helping Teens

`http://www.ldteens.org`

This site was developed by teens with dyslexia to help others with dyslexia gain knowledge, a positive self-image, and a forum for expression. It also has sections for parents and teachers.

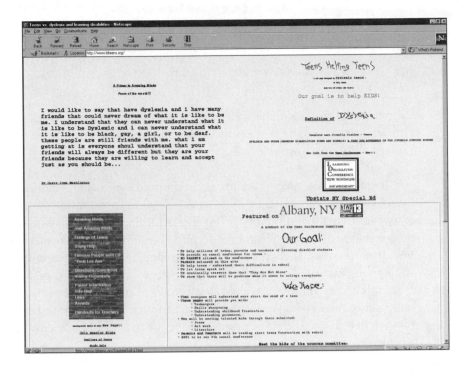

The Schwab Foundation for Learning

`http://www.schwablearning.org`

This foundation offers a wide range of services and information for parents and educators to support and promote the lives of children with learning differences.

Speech or Language Impairment   Speech or language impairment means a communication disorder, such as stuttering, impaired articulation, a language impairment, or a voice impairment, that adversely affects a child's educational performance.

National Center for Stuttering

`http://www.stuttering.com`

The National Center For Stuttering provides factual information about stuttering, a National Stutterer's Hotline, treatment for small groups of selected individuals who stutter, continuing education for speech pathologists, and research into the causes and treatment of stuttering.

Net Connections for Communication Disorders and Sciences

```
http://www.mankato.msus.edu/dept/comdis/kuster2/
welcome.html
```

Resources for professionals and students in communication disorders and sciences as well as for persons with communication disabilities and those who are part of their lives.

Traumatic Brain Injury   Traumatic brain injury means an acquired injury to the brain caused by an external physical force, resulting in total or partial functional disability or psychosocial impairment, or both. The term applies to open or closed head injuries resulting in impairments in one or more areas, such as cognition; language; memory; attention; reasoning; abstract thinking; judgment; problem-solving; sensory, perceptual, and motor abilities; psychosocial behavior; physical functions; information processing; and speech. The term does not apply to brain injuries that are congenital or degenerative, or to brain injuries induced by birth trauma.

The Brain Injury Association, Inc.

```
http://www.biausa.org
```

Prevention, treatment and rehabilitation, kid's corner, living life after a brain injury, many resources including books, tapes, videos, and links to other Web sites.

Curry School of Education Resources on Traumatic Brain Injury

```
http://curry.edschool.virginia.edu/go/cise/ose/
categories/tbi.html
```

The Whole Brain Atlas

```
http://www.med.harvard.edu/AANLIB/home.html
```

Harvard Medical Center presents a collection of images of human brains; contains a guided tour of neuroimaging and sections explaining the normal brain, as well as various medical conditions from Alzheimer's to stroke.

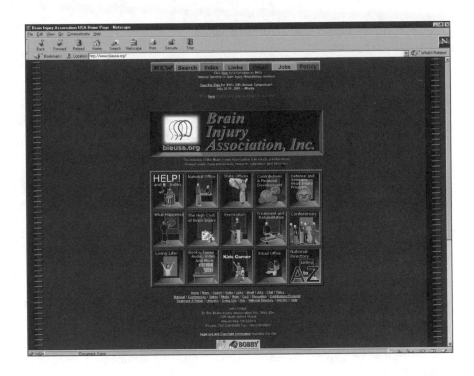

part

2

Visual Impairment Including Blindness   Visual impairment including blindness means an impairment in vision that, even with correction, adversely affects a child's educational performance. The term includes both partial sight and blindness.

American Council of the Blind (ACB)

`http://www.acb.org`

ACB strives to improve the well being of people who are blind or visually impaired. This site offers *The Braille Forum* (a free monthly magazine), forums, helpful resources, radio, programs, and more.

Assistive Technology for People Who Are Blind or Visually Impaired

`http://www.disabilityresources.org/AT-BLIND.html`

A Disability Resources Monthly guide to the best online resources about assistive technology for people who are blind or have visual impairments.

National Federation for the Blind

http://www.nfb.org

Links to news, events, research, jobline, resources.

STUDENTS WHO ARE GIFTED OR TALENTED

Giftedness is not a category of exceptionality under federal special education law. Nevertheless, several states provide specially designed instruction to students who are gifted and talented. There are many Web resources pertaining to giftedness that may be helpful to parents and teachers.

Belin & Blank International Center for Gifted Education and Talent Development

http://www.uiowa.edu/~belinctr

part

2

The State of Iowa Board of Regents established the center at the University of Iowa in June 1988. A leader in the field of gifted education, the center is known for its research, training, and service.

The Gifted and Talented Resources Home Page

http://www.eskimo.com/~user/kids.html

This Gifted Resources Page contains links to online gifted resources, enrichment programs, talent searches, summer programs, gifted mailing lists, and early acceptance programs. It also contains contact information for many local gifted associations and government programs.

National Association for Gifted Children

http://www.nagc.org

General information about NAGC, policy papers, publications and materials, parenting information, and state/federal information.

EARLY CHILDHOOD

States may provide special education services to children who are three through nine years old, not only under the categories of disability already described, but also if they are experiencing developmental delays in physical, cognitive, communication, social or emotional, or adaptive development.

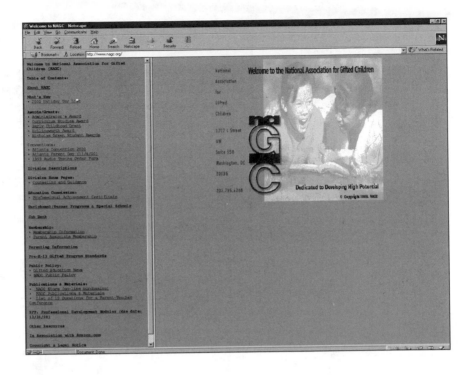

part

2

Division for Early Childhood, Council for Exceptional Children

http://www.dec-sped.org

Information for educators and families of young children with special needs; includes publications, conferences, legal information, and links to other sites.

National Early Childhood Technical Assistance System

http://www.nectas.unc.edu

NECTAS is a national technical assistance consortium working to support states, jurisdictions, and others to improve services and results for young children with disabilities and their families.

Toy Catalog Listing for Children with Special Needs

http://www.nas.com/downsyn/toy.html

Toys listed by title, links to producers; mailing list.

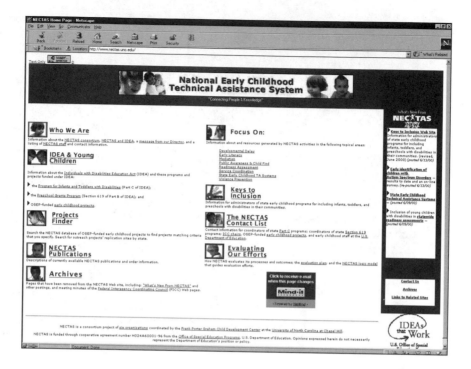

Zero to Three: National Center for Infants, Toddlers, and Families

http://www.zerotothree.org

Zero to three is an interactive Web site for parents and professionals. It includes a special section on how the brain develops, within the context of relationships, from conception through three years of age.

TRANSITION TO ADULTHOOD

Under the IDEA, transition services must be provided for students with disabilities to promote movement from school to post-school activities, including postsecondary education, vocational training, integrated employment (including supported employment), continuing and adult education, adult services, independent living, or community participation.

The DRM Guide to Disability Resources on the Internet

http://www.disabilityresources.org

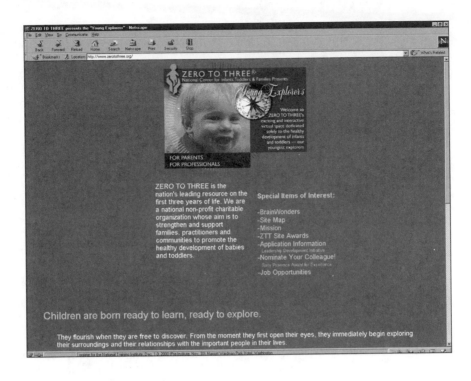

Disability Resources Monthly provides comprehensive and easy-to-find information on resources related to independent living.

HEATH Resource Center

http://www.acenet.edu/about/programs/Access&Equity/
HEATH/home.html

The HEATH Resource Center of the American Council on Education is the national clearinghouse on postsecondary education for individuals with disabilities. Support from the U.S. Department of Education enables HEATH to serve as an information exchange about educational support services, policies, procedures, adaptations, and opportunities at American campuses, vocational-technical schools, and other postsecondary training entities.

Job Accommodation Network

http://www.jan.wvu.edu

Service of the President's Committee on Employment of People with Disabilities; publications, facts about job accommodations.

part

2

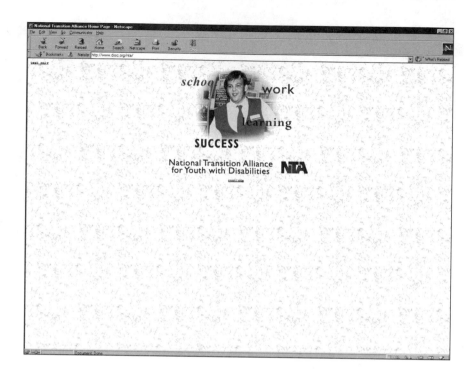

National Transition Alliance for Youth with Disabilities

http://www.dssc.org/nta

Publications, resources, searchable databases, model programs.

School to Career

http://www.sna.com/switp

The site includes information for students (It's About Your Life: What Students in Special Education Need to Know About the Transition Years) and many links to school and career resources, as well as information on disabilities.

The School to Work Outreach Project (STWOP)

http://www.ici.coled.umn.edu/schooltowork

STWOP, funded by the U.S. Department of Education, presents profiles of exemplary school-to-work models/practices/strategies.

Tools for Teachers

The Internet contains many tools for teachers. In it you can find resources for your classroom, lesson plans and ideas from seasoned teachers, as well as ideas for collaborating with other teachers, parents, and auxiliary support personnel (paraprofessionals, school psychologists, and medical professionals). You can also find tips for writing Individualized Education Programs (IEPs), developing behavior change plans and performing functional behavior analysis as required under federal law.

FUNCTIONAL BEHAVIORAL ANALYSIS AND BEHAVIORAL CHANGE PLANS

Under the discipline provisions of the 1997 Amendments to the IDEA, schools must address the problem behaviors of students with disabilities. The following Web sites provide assistance to educators in evaluating problem behavior and designing behavioral interventions.

part

2

Behavior Home Page

http://www.state.ky.us/agencies/behave/homepage.html

Contains legal information on the IDEA practices and regulations, behavioral interventions, and links to other sites, as well as a discussion forum. Modifications needed in a general education or self-contained classroom are also presented.

The Child Psychologist

http://www.childpsychology.com/fba_bip/index.htm

This Web site provides comprehensive information for IEP teams on functional behavioral assessment and behavior intervention plans.

Functional Behavior Assessment Mini Web

http://www.air-dc.org/cecp/fba/default.htm

An IEP team's introduction to functional behavior assessment and behavior change plans; how to conduct a functional behavior assessment.

Multimodal Functional Behavioral Assessment Behavior Intervention Plans

http://mfba.duq.edu

This site provides an introduction to functional behavioral assessment online.

PLANNING AND IMPLEMENTING INDIVIDUALIZED EDUCATION PROGRAMS

Developing the IEP: Putting the Pieces Together

http://nde4.nde.state.ne.us/SPED/iepproj/develop/
dindex.html

Wondering about the difference between a benchmark and an objective? How to write present level statements or annual goals? In this site the Nebraska Department of Education presents a technical assistance guide for teachers, which explains the major aspects of IEP development.

part

2

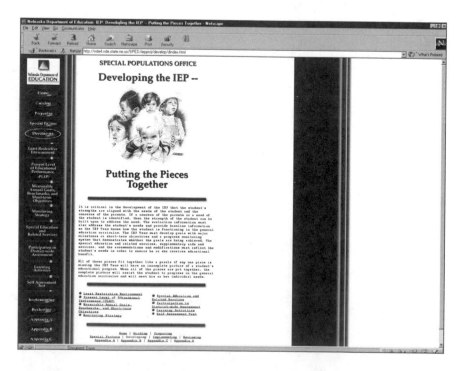

Guidelines for Completing the Sample IEP

http://web.nysed.gov/vesid/iep98007.htm

The New York State Education Department explains the IEP in depth.

The DRM WebWatcher: Individualized Education Programs (IEPs)

http://www.disabilityresources.org/IEP.html

This site provides links to help general education teachers, special education teachers, administrators, and counselors develop an IEP.

LD in Depth: Individualized Education Program

http://www.ldonline.org/ld_indepth/iep/iep.html

This site contains many links to help parents and teachers develop an IEP.

INCLUSION RESOURCES

part
2

Federal laws mandate that students with disabilities be integrated with nondisabled students to the maximum extent appropriate. The word "inclusion," which is not a legal term, is a synonym for integration of children with disabilities.

Circle of Inclusion

http://circleofinclusion.org

A Web site for early childhood service providers and families of young children with disabilities provides information about effective practices of inclusive educational programs for your children.

Institute on Community Integration

http://www.ici.coled.umn.edu/ici

Research, training, publications, resources.

The Inclusion Network

http://inclusion.org

The Inclusion Network is a Cincinnati-based nonprofit group with the goal of increasing integration of persons with disabilities at school, at

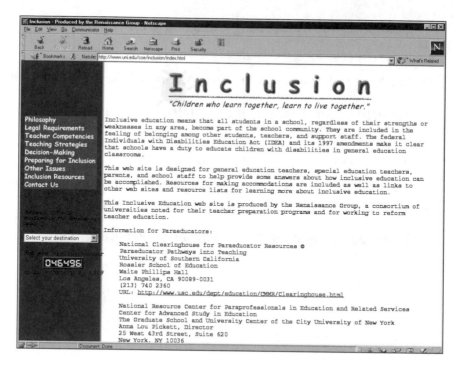

work, and in their communities. Provides background information on inclusion including the legislative mandates for inclusion. An inspirational site!

The What's and How To's of Inclusive Education

http://www.uni.edu/coe/inclusion/index.html

Provides current inclusion issues for general education and special education teachers. This site also provides resources for making accommodations. "Children who learn together, learn to live together."

LESSON PLANS AND MORE

21st Century Schoolhouse

http://www.coedu.usf.edu/~morris

Activities which accommodate different intelligences in the classroom; categories of information include educational links, newspapers in education, lesson plans, and spelling ticklers.

AskERIC

`http://ericir.syr.edu`

Need to know the latest information on special education, curriculum development or other education topics? Just AskERIC! When you submit your education question to Q&A, you'll receive a personal email within two business days! The virtual library contains selected educational resources, including lesson plans, InfoGuides, searchable archives of education-related listservs, links to television series companion guides, and much more! The ERIC database, the world's largest source of education information, contains more than one million abstracts of documents and journal articles on education research and practice.

Blue Web'n

`http://www.kn.pacbell.com/wired/bluewebn`

A library of Blue Ribbon learning sites on the Web. Reviews and provides links to hundreds and hundreds of lesson plans, activities, projects, references, and other resources on the Internet.

part
2

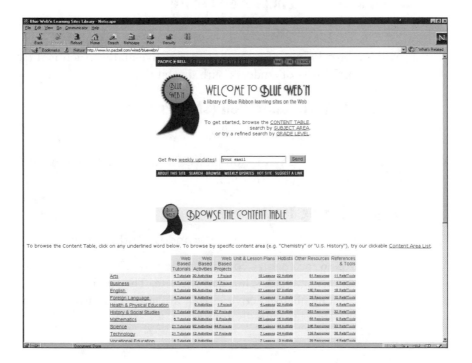

Education World

http://www.education-world.com

Searchable database of more than 50,000 sites related to curriculum ideas. Many resources are geared specifically toward children with exceptionalities.

Homework Central, Jr.

http://www.homeworkcentral.com

A resource for anyone interested in learning about disabilities. The site offers teachers and parents guidelines on identifying children with learning and physical disabilities. It also provides lesson plans with modifications to assist the general education teacher.

Kathy Schrock's Guide for Educators

http://school.discovery.com/schrockguide

A categorized list of sites on the Internet useful for enhancing curriculum and teacher professional growth.

National Center to Improve Practice

http://www2.edc.org/NCIP

Provides a broad range of resources on assistive and instructional technologies for teachers of students with disabilities.

The Special Needs Education (SNE) Project

http://www.schoolnet.ca/sne

Provides resources such as lesson plans, diagnostic tools, and other teaching and learning information.

Teachers Helping Teachers

http://www.pacificnet.net/~mandel/index.html

Teachers around the country contribute the activities, for students from kindergarten through high school, to this site. The special education section contains a number of activities that are geared toward teaching basic skills to students with disabilities.

part

2

ASSISTIVE TECHNOLOGY FOR STUDENTS WITH DISABILITIES

Abledata

http://www.abledata.com

ABLEDATA is a service of The National Institute on Disability and Rehabilitation Research (U.S. Department of Education). Looking for an assistive technology product? Whether it's a simple, low-tech device or a sophisticated computerized product, you'll probably find it in ABLEDATA's searchable database of approximately 23,000 assistive devices. You'll also find some invaluable fact sheets, consumer guides, and related material on this Web site.

Alliance for Technology Access

http://www.ataccess.org

Grassroots national organization to provide information/resources to parents and professionals on disabilities and technology.

Apple Disability Resources

http://www.apple.com/education/k12/disability

This site features a software library of freeware and shareware, a database of hundreds of disability products for the Macintosh, and information on Macintosh technologies.

Closing the Gap

http://www.closingthegap.com

Resource Guide to software and hardware, newspaper, articles, conferences related to computer technology in special education and rehabilitation.

Dreamms for Kids

http://www.dreamms.org

This assistive technology information clearinghouse is committed to increasing the use of computers and assistive technologies for students with special needs. The site has articles and products for special needs.

part
2

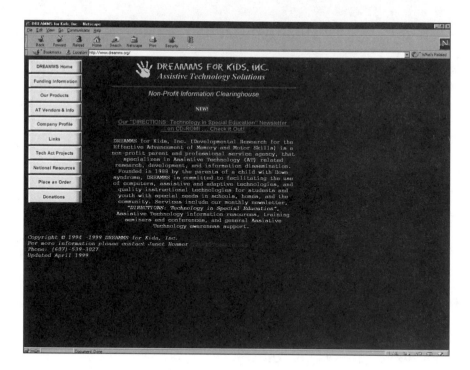

Microsoft's Accessibility Web Site

http://www.microsoft.com/enable/default.htm

Information on technology and accessibility aids such as screen enlargers, screen reviews, on-screen keyboards, and voice input devices.

Recording for the Blind and Dyslexic

http://www.rfbd.org

RFBD is a national nonprofit organization that serves people who cannot read standard print because of a visual, perceptual, or other physical disability. The site includes an online catalogue of books and how to get involved as a reader. There are also many links to additional information about visual impairments and other disabilities.

RESOURCES FOR PARENTS AND FAMILIES

Family & Advocates Partnership in Education (FAPE)

http://www.fape.org

FAPE aims to inform and educate families about the Individuals with Disabilities Education Act of 1997. This site has information on FAPE's goals, a calendar, laws and regulations, associated links, and more.

Family Education Network (FEN)

`http://familyeducation.com`

In partnership with the Council for Exceptional Children (CEC), the Family Education Network addresses the needs and concerns of parents of exceptional children and the educators who serve them. FEN is an online community of parents, teachers, and school dedicated to children's learning. The network includes *familyeducation.com* for parents, *teachervision.com* for teachers, and *myschoolonline.com* for school-home communication.

Family Village

`http://www.familyvillage.wisc.edu`

A global community of information, resources, and communication opportunities for persons with mental retardation and other disabilities;

part 2

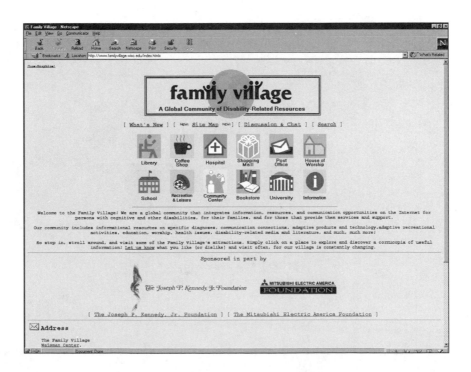

includes informational resources on specific disabilities, communication connections, adaptive products and technology, adaptive recreational activities, education, worship, health issues, disability-related media and literature, and much, much more.

Federation for Children with Special Needs

http://www.fcsn.org/home.htm

Massachusetts-based resource center for parents, project, updates.

National Fathers Network

http://www.fathersnetwork.org

NFN, a nonprofit organization providing support and resources to fathers and families with special needs children, provides articles, resources, links, and a photo album at their site.

part

2

National Information Center for Children and Youth with Disabilities (NICHCY)

http://www.nichcy.org

The National Information Center for Children and Youth with Disabilities is the national information and referral center that provides information on disabilities and disability-related issues for families, educators, and other professionals.

National Parent Information Network

http://www.npin.org

NPIN is a project of the ERIC system which is administered by the National Library of Education in the U.S. Department of Education; parent news, searchable database; a virtual library with full-text articles, summaries of books, and descriptions of newsletters and magazines.

Parents Helping Parents

http://www.php.com

National parent resource center, programs, events, links.

The Sibling Support Project

http://www.seattlechildrens.org/sibsupp//default.htm

The Sibling Support Project is a national program dedicated to the interests of brothers and sisters of people with special health and developmental needs. The project is based at Children's Hospital and Regional Medical Center in Seattle, Washington.

part
2

PROFESSIONAL ORGANIZATIONS

American Academy on Pediatrics

http://www.aap.org

Read the guidelines of the national professional organization of pediatricians on the diagnosis of Attention Deficit Disorder.

American Association of University Affiliated Programs for Persons with Developmental Disabilities

http://www.aauap.org

Authorized by the Developmental Disabilities Assistance and Bill of Rights Act (PL 104-183), UAPs are found in every state and territory of the U.S. Each is affiliated with a major research university. Visit this Web site to see what they have to offer in the way of academic training, technical assistance, services to the community, and research projects.

American Association on Mental Retardation

http://www.aamr.org

AAMR is a professional advocacy organization that was founded in 1876 to deal with life issues of persons with mental retardation. Its mission is to promote global development and dissemination of progressive policies, sound research, effective practices, and universal human rights for people with intellectual disabilities. Non-members can read old copies of the newsletter, visit the bookstore, or participate in online discussions.

American Psychological Association

http://www.apa.org/

Based in Washington, DC, the American Psychological Association (APA) is the largest scientific and professional organization representing psychology in the United States. APA is also the largest association of psychologists worldwide. The Web site contains many resources for the public and for students. Software on APA style of writing is available online for new writers in the behavioral sciences.

American Speech-Language-Hearing Association

http://www.asha.org

ASHA is the professional, scientific, and credentialing association for more than 97,000 audiologists, speech-language pathologists, and speech, language, and hearing scientists. This site is a resource for ASHA members, persons interested in information about communication disorders, and for those wanting career and membership information.

Association on Higher Education and Disability (AHEAD)

http://www.ahead.org

AHEAD is an organization of professionals committed to full participation in higher education for persons with disabilities.

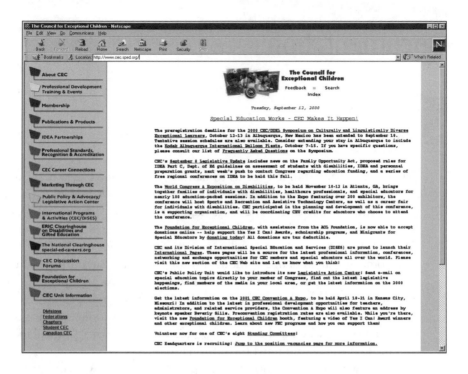

The Council for Exceptional Children

http://www.cec.sped.org

The Council for Exceptional Children (CEC) is the largest international professional organization dedicated to improving educational outcomes for individuals with exceptionalities, students with disabilities, and/or the gifted. CEC advocates for appropriate governmental policies, sets professional standards, provides continual professional development, advocates for newly and historically underserved individuals with exceptionalities, and helps professionals obtain conditions and resources necessary for effective professional practice.

The Council for Learning Disabilities

http://www.cldinternational.org

CLD International is an organization of professionals from diverse disciplines committed to the lifespan service of individuals with learning disabilities.

Documentation

Your Citation for Exemplary Research

There's another detail left for us to handle—the formal citing of electronic sources in academic papers. The very factor that makes research on the Internet exciting is the same factor that makes referencing these sources challenging: their dynamic nature. A journal article exists, either in print or on microfilm, virtually forever. A document on the Internet can come, go, and change without warning. Because the purpose of citing sources is to allow another scholar to retrace your argument, a good citation allows a reader to obtain information from your primary sources, to the extent possible. This means you need to include not only information on when a source was posted on the Internet (if available) but also when you obtained the information.

part

2

The two arbiters of form for academic and scholarly writing are the Modern Language Association (MLA) and the American Psychological Association (APA); both organizations have established styles for citing electronic publications.

MLA Style

In the fifth edition of the *MLA Handbook for Writers of Research Papers,* the MLA recommends the following formats:

- **URLs:** URLs are enclosed in angle brackets (<>) and contain the access mode identifier, the formal name for such indicators as "http" or "ftp." If a URL must be split across two lines, break it only after a slash (/). Never introduce a hyphen at the end of the first line. The URL should include all the parts necessary to identify uniquely the file/document being cited.

  `<http://www.csun.edu/~rtvfdept/home/index.html>`

- **An online scholarly project or reference database:** A complete online reference contains the title of the project or database (underlined); the name of the editor of the project or database (if given);

electronic publication information, including version number (if relevant and if not part of the title), date of electronic publication or latest update, and name of any sponsoring institution or organization; date of access; and electronic address.

The Perseus Project. Ed. Gregory R. Crane.
    Mar. 1997. Department of Classics, Tufts University. 15 June 1998 <http://www.perseus.tufts.edu/>.

If you cannot find some of the information, then include the information that is available. The MLA also recommends that you print or download electronic documents, freezing them in time for future reference.

- **A document within a scholarly project or reference database:** It is much more common to use only a portion of a scholarly project or database. To cite an essay, poem, or other short work, begin this citation with the name of the author and the title of the work (in quotation marks). Then, include all the information used when citing a complete online scholarly project or reference database, however, make sure you use the URL of the specific work and not the address of the general site.

part
2

Cuthberg, Lori. "Moonwalk: Earthlings' Finest Hour."
    Discovery Channel Online. 1999. Discovery
    Channel. 25 Nov. 1999 <http://www.discovery.com/
    indep/newsfeatures/moonwa lk/challenge.html>.

- **A professional or personal site:** Include the name of the person creating the site (reversed), followed by a period, the title of the site (underlined), or, if there is no title, a description such as Home page (such a description is neither placed in quotes nor underlined). Then, specify the name of any school, organization, or other institution affiliated with the site and follow it with your date of access and the URL of the page.

Packer, Andy. Home page. 1 Apr. 1998
    <http://www.suu.edu/~students/Packer.htm>.

Some electronic references are truly unique to the online domain. These include email, newsgroup postings, MUDs (multiuser domains) or MOOs (multiuser domains, object-oriented), and IRCs (Internet Relay Chats).

Email   In citing email messages, begin with the writer's name (reversed) followed by a period, then the title of the message (if any) in quotations as it appears in the subject line. Next comes a description of the message, typically "Email to," and the recipient (e.g., "the author"), and finally the date of the message.

```
Davis, Jeffrey. "Web Writing Resources." Email to
     Nora Davis. 3 Jan. 2000.
```

```
Sommers, Laurice. "Re: College Admissions Practices."
     Email to the author. 12 Aug. 1998.
```

List Servers and Newsgroups   In citing these references, begin with the author's name (reversed) followed by a period. Next include the title of the document (in quotes) from the subject line, followed by the words "Online posting" (not in quotes). Follow this with the date of posting. For list servers, include the date of access, the name of the list (if known), and the online address of the list's moderator or administrator. For newsgroups, follow "Online posting" with the date of posting, the date of access, and the name of the newsgroup, prefixed with "news:" and enclosed in angle brackets.

```
Applebaum, Dale. "Educational Variables." Online
     posting. 29 Jan. 1998. Higher Education
     Discussion Group. 30 Jan. 1993
     <jlucidoj@unc.edu>.
```

```
Gostl, Jack. "Re: Mr. Levitan." Online posting.
     13 June 1997. 20 June 1997
     <news:alt.edu.bronxscience>.
```

MUDs, MOOs, and IRCs   Begin with the name of the speaker(s) followed by a period. Follow with the description and date of the event, the forum in which the communication took place, the date of access, and the online address. If you accessed the MOO or MUD through telnet, your citation might appear as follows:

```
Guest. Personal interview. 13 Aug. 1998.
     <telnet://du.edu:8888>.
```

For more information on MLA documentation style for online sources, check out their Web site at http://www.mla.org/style/sources.htm.

part

2

APA Style

The *Publication Manual of the American Psychological Association* (4th ed.) is fairly dated in its handling of online sources, having been published before the rise of the WWW and the generally recognized format for URLs. The format that follows is based on the APA manual, with modifications. It's important to remember that, unlike the MLA, the APA does not include temporary or transient sources (e.g., letters, phone calls, etc.) in its "References" page, preferring to handle them in in-text citations exclusively. This rule holds for electronic sources as well: email, MOOs/MUDs, list server postings, etc., are not included in the "References" page, merely cited in text, for example, "But Wilson has rescinded his earlier support for these policies" (Charles Wilson, personal email to the author, 20 November 1996). But also note that many list server and Usenet groups and MOOs actually archive their correspondences, so that there is a permanent site (usually a Gopher or FTP server) where those documents reside. In that case, you would want to find the archive and cite it as an unchanging source. Strictly speaking, according to the APA manual, a file from an FTP site should be referenced as follows:

```
Deutsch, P. (1991). Archie: An electronic directory
    service for the Internet [Online]. Available FTP:
    ftp.sura.net Directory: pub/archie/docs File:
    whatis.archie.
```

part 2

However, the increasing familiarity of Net users with the convention of a URL makes the prose description of how to find a file ("Available FTP: ftp.sura.net Directory: pub/archie/docs File: whatis.archie") unnecessary.

So, with modification of the APA format (as suggested by the APA at its Web page www.apa.org/journals/webref.html), citations from the standard Internet sources would appear as follows.

FTP (File Transfer Protocol) Sites To cite files available for downloading via FTP, give the author's name (if known), the publication date (if available and if different from the date accessed), the full title of the paper (capitalizing only the first word and proper nouns), the date of access, and the address of the FTP site along with the full path necessary to access the file.

```
Deutsch, P. (1991) Archie: An electronic directory
    service for the Internet. Retrieved January 25,
    2000 from File Transfer Protocol: ftp://
    ftp.sura.net/pub/archie/docs/whatis.archie
```

WWW Sites (World Wide Web) To cite files available for viewing or downloading via the World Wide Web, give the author's name (if known), the year of publication (if known and if different from the date accessed), the full title of the article, and the title of the complete work (if applicable) in italics. Include any additional information (such as versions, editions, or revisions) in parentheses immediately following the title. Include the date of retrieval and full URL (the http address).

```
Burka, L. P. (1993). A hypertext history of multi-
    user dungeons. MUDdex. Retrieved January 13, 1997
    from the World Wide Web: http://www.utopia.com/
    talent/lpb/muddex/essay/
```

```
Tilton, J. (1995). Composing good HTML (Vers. 2.0.6).
    Retrieved December 1, 1996 from the World Wide Web:
    http://www.cs.cmu.edu/~tilt/cgh/
```

part

2

Synchronous Communications (MOOs, MUDs, IRC, etc.) Give the name of the speaker(s), the complete date of the conversation being referenced in parentheses, and the title of the session (if applicable). Next, list the title of the site in italics, the protocol and address (if applicable), and any directions necessary to access the work. Last, list the date of access, followed by the retrieval information. Personal interviews do not need to be listed in the References, but do need to be included in parenthetic references in the text (see the APA *Publication Manual*).

```
Cross, J. (1996, February 27). Netoric's Tuesday
    cafe: Why use MUDs in the writing classroom?
    MediaMoo. Retrieved March 1, 1996 from File
    Transfer Protocol: ftp://daedalus.com/
    pub/ACW/NETORIC/catalog
```

Gopher Sites List the author's name (if applicable), the year of publication, the title of the file or paper, and the title of the complete work (if applicable). Include any print publication information (if available) followed by the protocol (i.e., gopher://). List the date that the file was accessed and the path necessary to access the file.

```
Massachusetts Higher Education Coordinating Council.
    (1994). Using coordination and collaboration to
    address change. Retrieved July 16, 1999 from the
    World Wide Web: gopher://gopher.mass.edu:170/
    00gopher_root%3A%5B_hecc%5D_plan
```

Email, Listservs, and Newsgroups Do not include personal email in the list of References. Although unretrievable communication such as email is not included in APA References, somewhat more public or accessible Internet postings from newsgroups or listservs may be included. See the APA *Publication Manual* for information on in-text citations.

```
Heilke, J. (1996, May 3). Webfolios. Alliance for
    Computers and Writing Discussion List. Retrieved
    December 31, 1996 from the World Wide Web:
    http://www.ttu.edu/lists/acw-l/9605/0040.html
```

Other authors and educators have proposed similar extensions to the APA style, too. You can find URLs to these pages at

```
www.psychwww.com/resource/apacrib.htm
```

Another frequently-referenced set of extensions is available at

```
www.uvm.edu/ncrane/estyles/apa.htm
```

Remember, "frequently-referenced" does not equate to "correct" or even "desirable." Check with your professor to see if your course or school has a preference for an extended APA style.

part

2

appendix

Listing of Web Sites by Section

Why Are the Internet and the World Wide Web Important for Special Education?

We Media: The Disability Network

http://www.wemedia.com

American Hyperlexia Association

http://www.hyperlexia.org

Rett Syndrome

http://www.isn.net/~jypsy/rett.htm

Angelman Syndrome Foundation

http://www.angelman.org

Williams Syndrome Association

http://www.williams-syndrome.org

The Educational Resources Information Center

http://www.accesseric.org/

ERIC Clearinghouse on Disabilities and Gifted Education

`http://ericec.org`

The Internet as a Tool for Your Studies in Special Education

HISTORICAL AND PHILOSOPHICAL BACKGROUND OF SPECIAL EDUCATION

Special Education as an Outgrowth of the Civil Rights Movement

Disability Social History Project

`http://www.disabilityhistory.org/dshp.html`

appendix

Non-Labeling Language

Disability Etiquette Handbook

`http://www.ci.sat.tx.us/planning/handbook/`

People First Language

`http://www.kidstogether.org/pep-1st.htm`

The Utterly Adaptable Etiquette Guide

`http://www.labor.state.ut.us/`
`Utah_Antidiscrimination___Labo/defdis/etiquett/`
`etiquett.htm`

Words with Dignity

`http://www.paraquad.org/wwd.htm`

Special Education Terminology

Alphabet Soup: Disability Related Acronyms

`http://www.disabilityresources.org/ABC.html`

Glossary of Special Ed Terms

`http://www.disabilityrights.org/glossary.htm`

The Special Educator as Advocate

Code of Ethics and Standards of Practice for Educators of Persons with Exceptionalities

`http://www.cec.sped.org/ps/code.htm`

The Disability Rights Activist

`http://disrights.org`

Disability Rights Education and Defense Fund

`http://www.dredf.org`

appendix

The National Association of Protection and Advocacy Systems

`http://protectionandadvocacy.com`

Wrightslaw: The Special Ed Advocate

`http://www.wrightslaw.com`

LEGAL ASPECTS OF EDUCATING STUDENTS WITH EXCEPTIONALITIES

The Individuals with Disabilities Education Act (IDEA)

Idea Practices

`http://www.ideapractices.org`

IDEA '97

`http://www.ed.gov/offices/OSERS/IDEA/index.html`

Section 504 of the Vocational Rehabilitation Act

Federal Requirements for Free Appropriate Public Education under Section 504

http://www.ed.gov/offices/OCR/fape.html

Section 504 and Education

http://www.ed.gov/offices/OCR/ocr504.html

The Americans with Disabilities Act (ADA)

Americans with Disabilities Act Document Center

http://janweb.icdi.wvu.edu/kinder/index.htm

appendix

U.S. Department of Justice ADA Home Page

http://www.usdoj.gov/crt/ada/adahom1.htm

Section 504 and IDEA: Basic Similarities and Differences

http://www.edlaw.net/service/504idea.html

Comparative Analysis: IDEA, Section 504 and the ADA

http://at-advocacy.phillynews.com/misc/cohen2.html

Government

Office of Special Education and Rehabilitative Services

http://www.ed.gov/offices/OSERS

Office of Special Education Programs

http://www.ed.gov/offices/OSERS/OSEP/index.html

The Rehabilitation Services Administration

http://www.ed.gov/offices/OSERS/RSA/index.html

The National Institute on Disability and Rehabilitation Research

http://www.ed.gov/offices/OSERS/NIDRR/

The Supreme Court

The Oyez Project

http://oyez.nwu.edu

The Cornell University Law Library

http://www.law.cornell.edu/supct/

DOCUMENTING ELECTRONIC SOURCES IN YOUR SCHOLARLY WRITING

appendix

APA Style Resources

http://www.psychwww.com/resource/apacrib.htm

Electronic Reference Formats Recommended by the APA

http://www.apa.org/journals/webref.html

A Guide for Writing Research Papers Based on Styles Recommended by the APA

http://webster.commnet.edu/apa/apa_index.htm

INFORMATION ON SPECIFIC DISABILITIES

Special Education Resources on the Internet (SERI)

http://www.hood.edu/seri

Autism

Autism Research Institute (ARI)

http://www.autism.com/ari/

Autism Society of America (ASA)

http://www.autism-society.org

Center for the Study of Autism

http://www.autism.org

Oops. . . . Wrong Planet Syndrome

http://www.isn.net/~jypsy/index.html

Deaf–Blindness

A–Z to Deaf–Blindness

http://www.deafblind.com

D–B Link: National Information Clearinghouse for Children Who Are Deaf–Blind

http://www.tr.wou.edu/dblink/index.htm

Helen Keller National Center for Deaf–Blind Youths and Adults

http://www.helenkeller.org/national/index.htm

Deafness

Alexander Graham Bell Association for the Deaf (AGBell)

http://www.agbell.org

Council on Education of the Deaf

http://www.educ.kent.edu/deafed

The Deaf Education Option Web

http://www2.pair.com/options/

Wallace Library Guides

http://wally.rit.edu/internet/subject/deafness.html

Emotional Disturbance

American Academy of Child and Adolescent Psychiatry

`http://www.aacap.org/`

Center for Effective Collaboration and Practice (CECP)

`http://cecp.air.org/index.htm`

Internet Mental Health

`http://www.mentalhealth.com`

National Association for the Mentally Ill

`http://www.nami.org/medical.htm`

Hearing Impairment

appendix

Alexander Graham Bell Association for the Deaf and Hard of Hearing

`http://www.agbell.org`

Hard of Hearing and Deaf Students: A Resource Guide to Support Classroom Teachers

`http://www.bced.gov.bc.ca/specialed/hearimpair/toc.htm`

Mental Retardation

National Down Syndrome Association

`http://www.ndss.org`

National Fragile X Foundation

`http://www.nfxf.org`

The Arc of the United States

`http://thearc.org`

Multiple Disabilities

Activity Ideas for Students with Severe/Profound/ Multiple Disabilities

http://www.palaestra.com/featurestory.html

The Association for Persons with Severe Disabilities

http://www.tash.org

Orthopedic Impairment

Information about Mobility Impairments

http://spot.pcc.edu/osd/mobinfo.htm

appendix

Muscular Dystrophy Association

http://www.mdausa.org

Strategies for Teaching Children with Motor/Orthopedic Impairments

http://www.as.wvu.edu/~scidis/motor.html

United Cerebral Palsy Association

http://www.ucpa.org

Other Health Impairment Including Attention Deficit Disorder

Band-aides and Blackboards: When Chronic Illness or Some Other Medical Problem Goes to School

http://funrsc.fairfield.edu/~jfleitas/sitemap.html

Candlelighters' Childhood Cancer Foundation

http://candlelighters.org

CHADD

http://www.chadd.org

Elizabeth Glaser Pediatric AIDS Foundation

`http://www.pedaids.org`

The Epilepsy Foundation

`http://www.efa.org`

The Foundation for Medically Fragile Children

`http://www.care4gakids.com/`

National Attention Deficit Disorder Association

`http://www.add.org`

National Organization for Rare Disorders (NORD)

`http://www.rarediseases.org/`

appendix

Specific Learning Disability

Dyslexia: The Gift

`http://www.dyslexia.com`

International Dyslexia Society

`http://www.interdys.org`

Internet Special Education Resources

`http://www.iser.com`

The Learning Disabilities Association of America

`http://www.ldanatl.org/`

LD Online

`http://www.ldonline.org`

National Center for Learning Disabilities, Inc.

`http://www.ncld.org`

Teens Helping Teens

http://www.ldteens.org

The Schwab Foundation for Learning

http://www.schwablearning.org

Speech or Language Impairment

National Center for Stuttering

http://www.stuttering.com

Net Connections for Communication Disorders and Sciences

http://www.mankato.msus.edu/dept/comdis/kuster2/
welcome.html

appendix

Traumatic Brain Injury

The Brain Injury Association, Inc.

http://www.biausa.org

Curry School of Education Resources on Traumatic Brain Injury

http://curry.edschool.virginia.edu/go/cise/ose/
categories/tbi.html

The Whole Brain Atlas

http://www.med.harvard.edu/AANLIB/home.html

Visual Impairment Including Blindness

American Council of the Blind (ACB)

http://www.acb.org

Assistive Technology for People Who are Blind or Visually Impaired

http://www.disabilityresources.org/AT-BLIND.html

National Federation for the Blind

http://www.nfb.org

Students Who Are Gifted or Talented

Belin & Blank International Center for Gifted Education and Talent Development

http://www.uiowa.edu/~belinctr

The Gifted and Talented Resources Home Page

http://www.eskimo.com/~user/kids.html

National Association for Gifted Children

http://www.nagc.org

appendix

EARLY CHILDHOOD

Division for Early Childhood, Council for Exceptional Children

http://www.dec-sped.org

National Early Childhood Technical Assistance System

http://www.nectas.unc.edu/

Toy Catalog Listing for Children with Special Needs

http://www.nas.com/downsyn/toy.html

Zero to Three: National Center for Infants, Toddlers, and Families

http://www.zerotothree.org/

TRANSITION TO ADULTHOOD

The DRM Guide to Disability Resources on the Internet

http://www.disabilityresources.org/

HEATH Resource Center

```
http://www.acenet.edu/about/programs/Access&Equity/
HEATH/home.html
```

Job Accommodation Network

```
http://www.jan.wvu.edu
```

National Transition Alliance for Youth with Disabilities

```
http://www.dssc.org/nta
```

School to Career

```
http://www.sna.com/switp
```

The School to Work Outreach Project (STWOP)

```
http://www.ici.coled.umn.edu/schooltowork
```

appendix

 Tools for Teachers

FUNCTIONAL BEHAVIORAL ANALYSIS AND BEHAVIORAL CHANGE PLANS

Behavior Home Page

```
http://www.state.ky.us/agencies/behave/homepage.html
```

The Child Psychologist

```
http://www.childpsychology.com/fba_bip/index.htm
```

Functional Behavior Assessment Mini Web

```
http://www.air-dc.org/cecp/fba/default.htm
```

Multimodal Functional Behavioral Assessment Behavior Intervention Plans

```
http://mfba.duq.edu/
```

PLANNING AND IMPLEMENTING INDIVIDUALIZED EDUCATION PROGRAMS

Developing the IEP: Putting the Pieces Together

http://nde4.nde.state.ne.us/SPED/iepproj/develop/
dindex.html

Guidelines for Completing the Sample IEP

http://web.nysed.gov/vesid/iep98007.htm

The DRM WebWatcher: Individualized Education Programs (IEPs)

http://www.disabilityresources.org/IEP.html

LD in Depth: Individualized Education Program

http://www.ldonline.org/ld_indepth/iep/iep.html

INCLUSION RESOURCES

Circle of Inclusion

http://circleofinclusion.org/

Institute on Community Integration

http://www.ici.coled.umn.edu/ici

The Inclusion Network

http://inclusion.org

The What's and How To's of Inclusive Education

http://www.uni.edu/coe/inclusion/index.html

appendix

LESSON PLANS AND MORE

21st Century Schoolhouse

http://www.coedu.usf.edu/~morris

AskERIC

http://ericir.syr.edu/

Blue Web'n

http://www.kn.pacbell.com/wired/bluewebn/

Education World

http://www.education-world.com

Homework Central, Jr.

http://www.homeworkcentral.com

Kathy Schrock's Guide for Educators

http://school.discovery.com/schrockguide

National Center to Improve Practice

http://www2.edc.org/NCIP/

The Special Needs Education (SNE) Project

http://www.schoolnet.ca/sne

Teachers Helping Teachers

http://www.pacificnet.net/~mandel/index.html

ASSISTIVE TECHNOLOGY FOR STUDENTS WITH DISABILITIES

ABLEDATA

http://www.abledata.com

Alliance for Technology Access

http://www.ataccess.org

Apple Disability Resources

http://www.apple.com/education/k12/disability/

Closing the Gap

http://www.closingthegap.com/

Dreamms for Kids

http://www.dreamms.org

Microsoft's Accessibility Web Site

http://www.microsoft.com/enable/default.htm

Recording for the Blind and Dyslexic

http://www.rfbd.org

RESOURCES FOR PARENTS AND FAMILIES

Family & Advocates Partnership in Education (FAPE)

http://www.fape.org

Family Education Network (FEN)

http://familyeducation.com

Family Village

http://www.familyvillage.wisc.edu

Federation for Children with Special Needs

http://www.fcsn.org/home.htm

appendix

National Fathers Network

http://www.fathersnetwork.org

The National Information Center for Children and Youth with Disabilities (NICHCY)

http://www.nichcy.org

National Parent Information Network

http://www.npin.org

Parents Helping Parents

http://www.php.com

The Sibling Support Project

http://www.seattlechildrens.org/sibsupp/default.htm

PROFESSIONAL ORGANIZATIONS

American Academy on Pediatrics

http://www.aap.org

American Association of University Affiliated Programs for Persons with Developmental Disabilities

http://www.aauap.org

American Association on Mental Retardation

http://www.aamr.org

American Psychological Association

http://www.apa.org/

American Speech-Language-Hearing Association

http://www.asha.org

Association on Higher Education and Disability (AHEAD)

`http://www.ahead.org`

The Council for Exceptional Children

`http://www.cec.sped.org`

The Council for Learning Disabilities

`http://www.cldinternational.org`

appendix

Glossary

Your Own Private Glossary

The Glossary in this book contains reference terms you'll find useful as you get started on the Internet. After a while, however, you'll find yourself running across abbreviations, acronyms, and buzzwords whose definitions will make more sense to you once you're no longer a novice (or "newbie"). That's the time to build a glossary of your own. For now, the 2DNet Webopædia gives you a place to start.

alias
A simple email address that can be used in place of a more complex one.

AVI
Audio Video Interleave. A video compression standard developed for use with Microsoft Windows. Video clips on the World Wide Web are usually available in both AVI and QuickTime formats.

bandwidth
Internet parlance for capacity to carry or transfer information such as email and Web pages.

browser
The computer program that lets you view the contents of Web sites.

client
A program that runs on your personal computer and supplies you with Internet services, such as getting your mail.

cyberspace
The whole universe of information that is available from computer networks. The term was coined by science fiction writer William Gibson in his novel *Neuromancer*, published in 1984.

DNS
See *domain name server.*

domain
A group of computers administered as a single unit, typically belonging to a single organization such as a university or corporation.

domain name
A name that identifies one or more computers belonging to a single domain. For example, "apple.com".

domain name server
A computer that converts domain names into the numeric addresses used on the Internet.

download
Copying a file from another computer to your computer over the Internet.

email
Electronic mail.

emoticon
A guide to the writer's feelings, represented by typed characters, such as the Smiley :-). Helps readers understand the emotions underlying a written message.

FAQs
Frequently Asked Questions

flame
A rude or derogatory message directed as a personal attack against an individual or group.

flame war
An exchange of flames (see above).

FTP
File Transfer Protocol, a method of moving files from one computer to another over the Internet.

home page
A page on the World Wide Web that acts as a starting point for information about a person or organization.

hypertext
Text that contains embedded *links* to other pages of text. Hypertext enables the reader to navigate between pages of related information by following links in the text.

LAN
Local Area Network. A computer network that is located in a concentrated area, such as offices within a building.

link
A reference to a location on the Web that is embedded in the text of the Web page. Links are usually highlighted with a different color or underlined to make them easily visible.

listserv
Strictly speaking, a computer program that administers electronic mailing lists, but also used to denote such lists or discussion groups, as in "the writer's listserv."

lurker
A passive reader of an Internet *newsgroup* or *listserv*. A lurker reads messages, but does not participate in the discussion by posting or responding to messages.

mailing list
A subject-specific automated email system. Users subscribe and receive email from other users about the subject of the list.

modem
A device for connecting two computers over a telephone line.

newbie
A new user of the Internet.

newsgroup
A discussion forum in which all participants can read all messages and public replies between the participants.

plug-in
A third-party software program that will lend a Web browser (Netscape, Internet Explorer, etc.) additional features.

quoted
Text in an email message or newsgroup posting that has been set off by the use of vertical bars or > characters in the left-hand margin.

search engine
A computer program that will locate Web sites or files based on specified criteria.

secure
A Web page whose contents are encrypted when sending or receiving information.

server

A computer program that moves information on request, such as a Web server that sends pages to your browser.

Smiley

See *emoticon.*

snail mail

Mail sent the old fashioned way: Write a letter, put it in an envelope, stick on a stamp, and drop it in the mailbox.

spam

Spam is to the Internet as unsolicited junk mail is to the postal system.

URL

Uniform Resource Locator: The notation for specifying addresses on the World Wide Web (e.g. http://www.abacon.com or ftp://ftp.abacon.com).

Usenet

The section of the Internet devoted to *newsgroups.*

Web browser

A program used to navigate and access information on the World Wide Web. Web browsers convert html coding into a display of pictures, sound, and words.

Web page

All the text, graphics, pictures, and so forth, denoted by a single URL beginning with the identifier "http://".

Web site

A collection of World Wide Web pages, usually consisting of a home page and several other linked pages.